FORMULA 1 2000

JEAN FRANÇOIS GALERON

© 2000, Chronosports Editeur
Jordils Park, Chemin des Jordils 40, CH-1025 St-Sulpice, Suisse.
Tél.: (+41 21) 697 14 14. Fax. (+41 21) 697 14 16

ISBN 1-85291-621-4
Published in Great Britain by Queen Anne Press
Mackerye End, Harpenden AL5 5DR

All text and photographs in this book are by Jean-Francois Galeron and from his archives.
The book was produced by Solange Amara, Sidonie Perrin, Aurelien Domont and Luc Domenjoz.
Printed in the European Union by Canale SpA/Torino, Italy.

Between the driver and his car...
all the expertise of Charmilles Technologies!

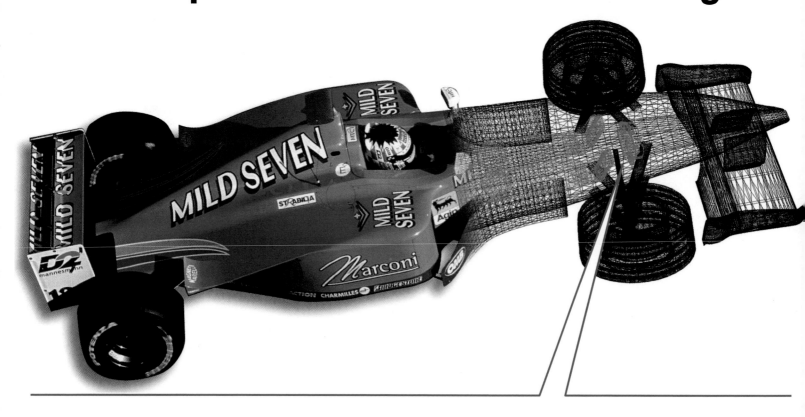

Accelerator pedal

This is a good illustration of the ease with which a complex part can be produced. The pedal was "recreated" thanks to the capacity of EDM wire cutting to machine thin surfaces with ease.
Result: reduced production time, improved sturdiness due to machining through the entire workpiece and, a crucial factor in Formula 1 racing, a marked weight saving.

To learn more about Charmilles Technologies' electrical discharge machining (EDM) and other Formula One parts used by West McLaren Mercedes, Benetton and Prost, such as gearbox pinions, steering racks, gear sticks, brake pedals, etc... request your copy of the brochure "F1 Partnerships" from Bruno Chambardon at the address opposite.

Brake pedal

A combination of EDM wire cutting for the contours and EDM die sinking to hollow out the interior.
Result: reduced production time and weight, married with enhanced rigidity.

Steering column

It is possible to produce steering column plates using conventional machining, but it is so much easier using programmable EDM to make the contours with fully automated machining, without the presence of an operator...
Result: saves time and simplifies production!

CHARMILLES TECHNOLOGIES

Charmilles Technologies S.A.
12, avenue du 1er mai
F - 91127 Palaiseau Cedex
Tél. 01 69 31 69 00
Fax 01 69 20 88 99
http://www.charmilles.com

AGIE CHARMILLES Group
GEORG FISCHER +GF+ Productique

Robofil 330F

FORMULA 1 2000

All text and photos by

JEAN FRANÇOIS GALERON

MELBOURNE
QANTAS
HEIDFELD
15
Formula 1
QANTAS
ALESI
14
QANTAS

Summary

Jean Francois Galeron would like to thank most sincerely, all the drivers who answered his questions and who put up with the being snapped at by his camera over the years.
Thanks also to all the press officers and team members, whose help and enthusiasm made his task so much easier.

PREFACE

Every Formula 1 driver dreams that one day he will get behind the wheel of a Ferrari. In fact, the first time I saw my name written on the side of the car when I did my first laps at Maranello, I experienced a very emotional moment. Luckily for my driving, the moment passed as soon as I flipped down the visor on my helmet.

I made my F1 debut back in 1993. That means I have spent seven years fighting and praying for a competitive car which would let me win races. Today, that dream has become reality. For me, this Ferrari is a gift from God. I hope that 2000 will be the best year of my career. I want to give back to Brazil, a real chance of winning.

Brazilians are once again as excited as they were in the days of Ayrton Senna. They cannot wait to have a fellow countryman with a real chance of winning and I have to put up with this pressure.

I think 2000 will be a thrilling season, not only for me, but also for Formula 1 as a whole. Race fans will be spoilt as there are at least four teams with a real chance of winning; something we have not seen for a long time.
We are going to live through incredible times.

The arrival of the major manufacturers, an ever increasing level of competitiveness, incredible use of technology, huge media interest and a growing television audience are the elements which make F1 today really magic.

I am very happy to write the preface to this book by my friend Jean-Francois Galeron, whom I have known since my debut in 1993. Just like me you will now have access to all those little secrets about Formula 1 in 2000 - the teams, drivers, circuits, statistics and all the fascinating details of this wonderful world which we love so much.

Maranello, 13th February 2000

Rubens Barrichello

From left to right and from top to bottom: Pedro Diniz, Mika Salo, Jenson Button, Ralf Schumacher, Eddie Irvine, Frentzen, Jarno Trulli, Marc Gené, Gaston Mazzacane, Giancarlo Fisichella, Alexander Wurz, David Coulthard,

Johnny Herbert, Jos Verstappen, Pedro De la Rosa, Jacques Villeneuve, Ricardo Zonta, Heinz-Harald
Mika Häkkinen, Michael Schumacher, Rubens Barrichello, Jean Alesi, Nick Heidfeld.

TEAMS AND DRIVERS

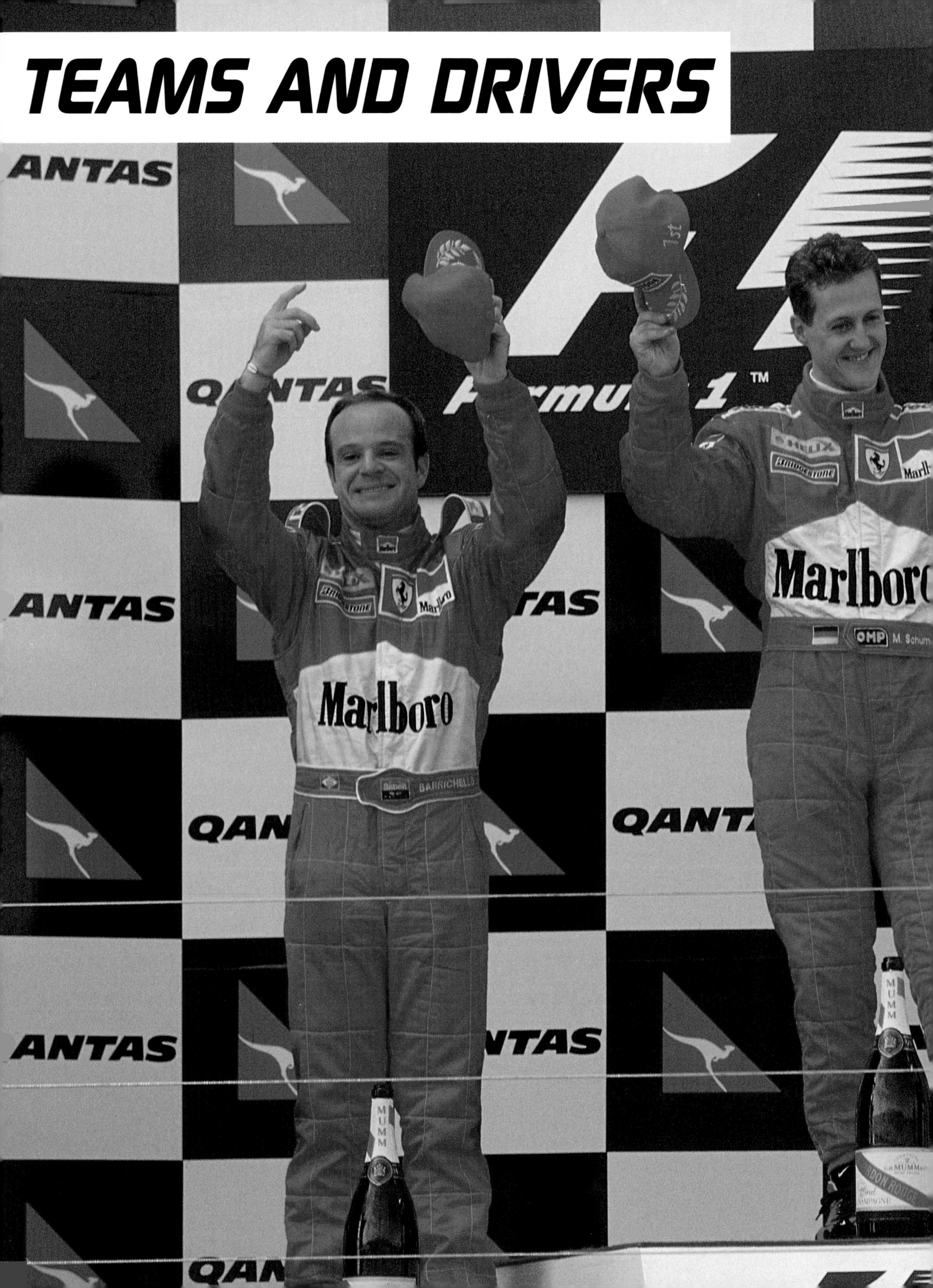

WEST McLAREN MERCEDES

ENGINE
Mercedes-Benz F0110 J V10
Number of cylinders : 72 degree V10
Capacity: 2998 cc
Power: 830 bhp
Weight: 98 kilos

Jerez, Thursday February 3, 2000. During the official launch of the McLaren MP4-15, a press release announces that the Daimler-Chrysler group has bought 40 per cent of the team. The power and health of this team are a watchword in Formula One. The technical and financial potential of its new partner is sure to maintain the team's superiority.
Ron Dennis, still the man in charge, isn't generous in defeat. He doesn't admit that Ferrari stole the Constructors' title from him last year.
Instead, he returns this year with redoubled motivation to regain what he feels is rightfully his. Everything at Woking has been put in place for this.
Mika Hakkinen and David Coulthard once again monopolised the front row of the grid at Melbourne. But the Silver Arrows, in spite of leading off the line, were prey to unreliability and allowed Ferrari to finish first and-second. The duel between the top two teams in the world had only just begun.

WEST McLAREN MERCEDES

McLaren Mercedes MP4-15
Tyres: Bridgestone
Address : McLaren International Ltd
Woking Business Park, Albert Drive
Woking, Surrey GU 21 5JY
England.
Tel : + 44 (0) 14 83 71 11 11
Fax : + 44 (0) 14 83 71 13 12
Web-site: www.mclaren.co.uk
Team principal: Ron Dennis
Technical director: Adrian Newey
Employees : 280
G.P. debut: Monaco 1966
G.P. participations: 492
First win: Belgium 1968 (B. McLaren)
Number of wins: 123
Number of pole positions : 103
Number of points scored: 2329.5 points
World Constructors' titles: 8 (1974, 84, 85, 88, 89, 90, 91 and 98)
World Drivers' titles: 11 (Fittipaldi 1974, Hunt 1976, Lauda 1984, Prost
1985, 86 and 89, Senna 1988, 90 and 91, Hakkinen 1998 and 99)
Third driver: Olivier Panis (France)
1999 position: 2nd (124 points)

Ron Dennis

Adrian Newey

- The team that sets the standard
- Same technical line-up
- Excellent Mercedes engine
- Great budget
- Mika Hakkinen
- Arrival of Olivier Panis
- 2000 car made more reliable

- Possible rivalry between drivers
- Dubious strategic ability

G.P. debut: USA 91 (Lotus)
World Drivers' champion in 1998 and 1999 (McLaren)
128 Grand Prix participations, 294 points scored, 14 wins, 21 pole positions
-1987 : Formula Ford champion (Finland, Sweden)
-1990 : Formula Three champion(GB)
F1 record:
-1991 : Lotus, 2 points, 15th in championship
-1992 : Lotus, 11 points, 8th in championship
-1993 : McLaren, (3 G.Ps. entered), 4 points, 15th in championship
-1994 : McLaren, 26 points, 4th in championship
-1995 : McLaren, 17 points, 7th in championship
-1996 : McLaren, 31 points, 5th in championship
-1997 : McLaren, 27 points, 5th in championship
-1998 : McLaren, 100 points, World Champion
-1999 : McLaren, 76 points, World Champion

Mika Häkkinen

West McLaren Mercedes

■ While Ayrton Senna remains the king of pole positions, certainly Mika Hakkinen could soon become his pretender. The Finnish driver excels in this area of racing, where you have to give the maximum over one lap. But the blonde Finn driver has more than one string to his bow. He's also gained a healthy appetite for winning World titles. After a long career where all success seemed to elude him, he's become addicted to winning.

After his great rival, Michael Schumacher's accident at Silverstone last year, one might have thought that winning his second World title would be easy. But that would be ignoring lady luck and the strongly impartial policy within the McLaren team which was scarcely favourable to his interests. Hakkinen had to wait until the final Grand Prix of the season in Japan to reap the fruits of his season, as he had the previous year.

Irvine, after Schumacher, couldn't prevent what at times seemed inevitable.

After long and well-deserved holidays, the two time World Champion returned this year stronger than ever. He can certainly count on the performance of his McLaren to help him to a third title, in spite of the inevitable Michael Schumacher who will do everything possible to prevent further domination.

First car driven?
A Mazda on my father knee in a forest. I was three years old.

Your personal car?
I have several Mercedes and a Ferrari 360. I'm sure that Michael Schumacher has a Mercedes. It's a very good way of learning your rivals' secrets

Favourite or dream car?
The Ferrari and McLaren road cars.

Most memorable race car?
The 1998 McLaren MP4-13.

Sweetest racing memory?
All my wins, and when I won the championships at Suzuka in 1998 and 1999.

Worst racing memory?
Imola 1994 and my accident in Adelaide in 1995.

Your favourite circuit?
Monaco, it's magic.

Your least favourite circuit?
Montreal.

Which driver from the past do you admire most?
None in particular.

Which current driver do you admire most?
No one at the moment.

Your favourite food?
It's a Finnish dish with meatballs

Favourite drink?
Water, tea, and Coca-Cola.

What sport do you do?
Running, swimming, skiing, tennis and jet-ski.

What are your favourite sports?
Alpine skiing, tennis and golf.

Who is your favourite sportsman?
The footballer Jari Litmanen, ski jumper Andreas Goldberger

and I have several good friends among the Finnish ice hockey players.

What are your hobbies?
Deep-sea diving and golf.

Your favourite films?
Horror films...

Favourite actors?
Bruce Willis, Schwarznegger and Stallone.

What do you watch on television?
Sports programmes.

What's your favourite colour?
Dark blue and black

Favourite music?
Dire Straits, Phil Collins, Michael Jackson and Mick Jagger.

What do you read?
Novels.

What is your goal in racing?
A third World Drivers' title!

Outside motor racing, whom do you admire?
My wife Erja.

If you had to be marooned on a desert island, who or what would you take with you?
A telephone and Erja.

What do you think is the most important thing in life?
Good health.

What is it that fascinates you about your profession?
The competition and driving.

What don't you like about it?
Accidents.

What are your best qualities?
Good humour.

What are your faults?
I don't like to be alone.

Have you thought what you are going to do after Formula One?
No, F1 takes up all my time at the moment.

Date of birth : 28 September 1968
Place : Helsinki (Finland)
Nationality : Finnish
Residence : Monte Carlo
Marital status : married to Erja
Height : 1.79 m
Weight : 69 kg
Web-site : www.mika.hakki-nen.com

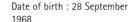

2

G.P. debut: Spain 1994
Best World Championship position: 3rd in 1995, in 1997 and in 1998
90 Grand Prix participations, 218 points scored, 6 wins, 8 pole positions
-1989 Junior Formula Ford Champion
F1 record:
-1994 : Williams, (8 G.Ps. entered), 14 points, 8th in championship
-1995 : Williams, 49 points, 3rd in championship
-1996 : McLaren, 18 points, 7th in championship
-1997 : McLaren, 36 points, 3rd in championship
-1998 : McLaren, 56 points, 3rd in championship
-1999 : McLaren, 45 points, 4th in championship

DAVID COULTHARD

West McLaren Mercedes

David Coulthard is at the crossroads. His average season in 1999 no doubt took its toll. The reliability of his McLaren could certainly have been better, and let him down on occasions. 'DC' as he's known in the paddock, was frequently unlucky. Certainly, his teammate Hakkinen suffered the same luck on occasions. But in spite of everything, he still had sufficient resources to claim a second World title. But how can one feel anything but a certain humiliation when faced with such success while using the same equipment?

Over the winter, the Scotsman has worked hard on two fronts. He has done a lot of testing, and he has forged a new approach. The presence of Olivier Panis, employed as third driver, has made him more determined to gain the required results.

Lack of reliability and one or two mistakes might well have dented his confidence. But he likes to remind people that "I'm 28 years old. At that age, Mika Hakkinen had already done more Grands Prix than I have today, and he still hadn't won. Why can't I be confident for the future?"

Ron Dennis always seeks equality for his drivers. In the past, Coulthard has often played the role of the ideal teammate. The McLaren MP4-15 is without doubt the car with which to fight with the best of them. Who says the likeable David, always available and smiling and one of the most friendly drivers in the paddock, might not be the man to beat this year?

First car driven?
I don't remember what the car was, I only remember that I was on my mother's knee and I was about eight or nine.

Your personal car?
My favourite is my 1971 Mercedes SEL convertible. I also have a Mercedes E 55 AMG.

Favourite or dream car?
It's still the McLaren F1 road car.

Most memorable race car?
The McLarens and the 1994 Williams.

Sweetest racing memory?
My win in Macau in F3.

Worst racing memory?
Last year, I had all sorts of problems. I made a mistake and went off at Nurburgring. I also want to forget Magny-Cours and Austria and my collision with Mika.

Your favourite circuit?
Spa, it's fantastic.

Your least favourite circuit?
I don't like Budapest.

Which driver from the past do you admire most?
Clark, Prost, Mansell and Senna.

Which current driver do you admire most?
None.

Your favourite food?
Pasta.

Favourite drink?
Tea and mineral water.

What sport do you do?
Golf, running, cycling and swimming.

What are your favourite sports?
Athletics.

Who is your favourite sportsman?
The athlete Lindford Christie.

What are your hobbies?
Living this life. Being with my fiancée Heidi, going to be sea, messing about in boats, seeing my family.

Your favourite films?
I love the cinema. I like action films like James Bond for instance. In my motorhome, I have a big screen so that I can watch my favourite films on video. Recently, I haven't had a lot of time to go to the movies, but I did see the latest James Bond recently.

Favourite actors?
Harrison Ford and the 'Indiana Jones', Stallone, Bruce Willis.

What do you watch on television?
I don't watch it.

What is your favourite colour?
Blue.

Favourite music?
Texas, Bon Jovi, Aerosmith, Guns and Roses, Queen, Phil Collins, The Corrs.

What do you read?
Nothing special.

What is your goal in racing?
Being an F1 driver was my dream.

Outside motor racing, whom do you admire?
Lindford Christie for his famous 100 meters, and Sean Connery in the role of James Bond.

If you had to be marooned on a desert island, who or what would you take with you?
My family and my fiancée Heidi.

What do you think is the most important thing in life?
Good health.

What fascinates you about your profession?
Speed.

What don't you like about it?
The politics and intrigue.

What are your best qualities?
You'll have to ask someone else!

What are your faults?
I've too many!

Have you thought what you are going to do after Formula One?
I think I'll carry on driving for another 20 years. After that, I don't know. I like the south of France, though.

Date of birth: March 27, 1971
Place: Twynholm (Scotland)
Nationality: British
Residence: Monte Carlo
Marital status: engaged to Heidi
Height: 1.82 m
Weight: 75 kg
Web-site: www.david.coulthard.com

ENGINE
V 10 049
Number of cylinders : 10 V 90 degree
Capacity: 2997 cc
Power : 830 bhp
Weight : 98 kilos

Slowly but surely, the Scuderia Ferrari is closing in on its ultimate target. After winning the 'minor' title of the Constructors' last year, it wants to add that of the Drivers' this year, a Championship that has eluded it for more than 20 years. Of course, with 'ifs' and 'buts' you can change everything, but if Michael Schumacher hadn't broken his leg at Silverstone last year, Ferrari might have already won both titles.

This year, Rubens Barrichello backs up the now recovered German driver.

This winter, yet again, Ferrari decided against any direct confrontation in testing with its rivals, preferring to test on home ground at Fiorano and Mugello. The F1-2000 is a more competitive evolution of last year's car.

At Melbourne, after McLaren's retirement, the Ferraris came home a powerful one-two. If that form is to be repeated everywhere, then the Prancing Horse could well be galloping away to those two World titles.

SCUDERIA FERRARI MARLBORO

Tyres: Bridgestone
Address: Gestione Sportiva
Scuderia Ferrari Marlboro
Via Ascari 55/57
41053 Maranello
Italy
Tel : + 39 0536 94 94 50
Fax : + 39 0536 94 94 36
Web-site: www.ferrari.it
Sporting Director: Jean Todt
Technical Director: Ross Brawn
Employees : 430
G. P. debut : Monaco 1950
G.P. participations : 618
First win: Britain 1951 (F. Gonzales)
Number of wins : 125
Number of pole positions : 127
Number of points scored: 2343.5 points
World Constructors' titles : 9 (1961, 64, 75, 76, 77, 79, 82, 83 and 99)
World Drivers' titles : 9 (Ascari 1952 and 1953, Fangio 1956,
Hawthorn 1958, P. Hill 1961, Surtees 1964, Lauda 1975 and 1977, Scheckter 1979)
Test driver : Luca Badoer (Italy)
1999 position: World Constructors' Champion (128 points)

Jean Todt

Ross Brawn

+	
- Huge budget	- Enormous pressure
- Same technical line-up	- Fiat financial state of health?
- Excellent race strategy	- Rivalry between the drivers?
- Michael Schumacher	- Reliability of the new engine?
- Arrival of Rubens Barrichello	
- No driver conflict	
- Good preparation programme	

G.P. debut : Belgium 1991 (Jordan)
128 Grand Prix participations, 570 points scored, 35 wins, 23 pole positions
World Drivers' champion in 1994 and 1995 (Benetton)
-1988 Formula Konig Champion of Germany
F1 record :
-1991 : Jordan and Benetton, 4 points, 12th in championship
-1992 : Benetton, 53 points, 3rd in championship
-1993 : Benetton, 52 points, 4th in championship
-1994 : Benetton, 92 points, World Champion
-1995 : Benetton, 102 points, World Champion
-1996 : Ferrari, 49 points, 3rd in championship
-1997 : Ferrari, 78 points, disqualified from championship
-1998 : Ferrari, 86 points, 2nd in championship
-1999 : Ferrari, (9 G.Ps. entered), 44 points, 5th in championship

MICHAEL SCHUMACHER

SCUDERIA FERRARI MARLBORO

Few people in this world are indifferent to Michael Schumacher. You either love him or hate him. But having won two titles with Benetton, at the beginning of the 1996 season he set himself the target of becoming World Champion with Ferrari. But he still hasn't managed it. This year is his fifth with the Scuderia. Last year, he might well have realised his dream, but for his accident. The challenge was put on hold again.

This year, the bookies in England make him clear favourite. He's as comfortable behind the wheel of his Ferrari as he was in a kart. This winter, he continued his recuperation first of all at his chalet in Norway, and later in Dubai, and he's now fully recovered from his Silverstone injuries. He's more motivated and competitive than ever, and after his long holiday, he could be totally dominant.

He was born to race, enlivens every race in which he drives, is constantly on the attack and has been a top driver now for ten years. He's surely the most popular driver in the world today. Half a Grand Prix crowd is there to see him. In Italy, they call him the 'Phenomenon.' His detractors are becoming more and more rare. When he hangs up his helmet, he will leave a void which will be hard to fill.

The older Schumacher is without doubt the best driver in the world today.

'The Red Baron' is one of the knights of the sport.

The day that Schumi brings the Drivers' title back to the tifosi will be one that will be celebrated throughout the land. Furthermore, this year the German driver is learning Italian.

First car driven?
A Fiat 500 when I was eight years old.

Your personal car?
A Maserati 3200 GT in Italy, an Alfa Romeo 166, a Lancia Zeta, a Ferrari 550 Maranello and a Fiat 500!

Favourite or dream car?
It doesn't exist.

Most memorable race car?
The 1994 Benetton and the Ferrari F 399 at the Malaysian GP in 1999.

Sweetest racing memory?
I like to be on the rostrum with my brother, as we were at Monza in 1998.
Last year, I had good memories of Imola and Sepang.

Worst racing memory?
Not my accident at Silverstone last year, but my collision with Villeneuve at Jerez in 1997.

Your favourite circuit?
Spa is my favourite.

Your least favourite circuit?
None.

Which driver from the past do you admire most?
Ayrton Senna.

Which current driver do you admire most?
My brother!

Your favourite food?
Italian food and spaghetti with tomato in particular.

Favourite drink?
Apple juice with sparkling water.

What sports do you do?
Karting, running, fitness training, cycling and mountain biking, deep sea diving and I play football with FC Aubonne in Switzerland when my current job allows me to.

What are your favourite sports?
I like all sports.

Who is your favourite sportsman?
Those who do decathlons and triathlons are more the most complete all-rounders.

What are your hobbies?
I enjoy playing with my children and filming them on video. I collect watches - mainly Omegas - and I like singing with karaoke.

Your favourite films?
The children's series 'Rudolf, the red nosed Reindeer', 'Titanic', 'The Silence of the Lambs' and 'La maison des esprits', and the films of Isabel Allende.
It's a shame I don't have more time to go to the cinema.

Favourite actors?
Jodie Foster, Meryl Streep, Nicolas Cage and Anthony Hopkins.

What do you watch on television?
News and good discussion programmes.

What's your favourite colour?
I don't have one.

Favourite music?
Phil Collins, Tina Turner, Michael Jackson and relaxing music.

What do you read?
Crime novels.

What is your goal in racing?
To win against tough opposition.

Outside motor racing, whom do you admire?
Triathletes for instance.

If you had to be marooned on a desert island, who or what would you take with you?
My wife Corinna and my two children.

What do you think is the most important thing in life?
My family.

What is it that fascinates you about your profession?
Working with my team, making progress and winning.

What don't you like about it?
When someone tries to hinder the work of the team.

What are your best qualities?
I don't like to talk about them.

What are your faults?
I count on you to tell me!

Have you thought what you are going to do after Formula One?
I think I will still be involved in motor sport. I will certainly have a role as ambassador for Fiat, and I already have a similar role with Unesco.

Date of birth : January 3 1969
Place : Huerth-Hermuelheim (Germany)
Nationality : German
Residence : Vuflens le Chateau (Switzerland)
Marital status : Married to Corinna, two children, Gina Maria and Mick
Height : 1.74 m
Weight : 74.5 kg
Web-site : www.michael-schumacher.de

G.P. debut : South Africa 1993
Best World Championship position : 6th in 1994
(Jordan)
113 Grand Prix participations, 71 points scored,
0 wins, 2 pole positions
-1990 Euroseries Opel Lotus champion
-1991 British F3 Champion
F1 record:
-1993 : Jordan, 2 points, 17th in championship
-1994 : Jordan, 19 points, 6th in championship
-1995 : Jordan, 11 points, 11th in championship
-1996 : Jordan, 14 points, 8th in championship
-1997 : Stewart, 6 points, 14th in championship
-1998 : Stewart, 4 points, 14th in championship
-1999 : Stewart, 21 points, 7th in championship

RUBENS BARRICHELLO

SCUDERIA FERRARI MARLBORO

Last year, Rubens Barrichello achieved good results driving the Stewart-Ford. He proved the extent of his talents both in qualifying and the race. But he's now also becoming one of the most experienced drivers in the field. So it's not just a matter of circumstances that Ferrari hired him to replace Eddie Irvine as teammate to Michael Schumacher. For 'Rubinho', of course, this was the realisation of a dream. He would finally have a car that would allow him to achieve what he had always dreamed of.

Calm and quiet, he doesn't want to be under the kind of pressure which he has avoided in his seven seasons so far. Having said that, he feels that the presence of the best driver in the world in the other Ferrari is extra motivation. In his native Brazil, his compatriots have forgotten the taste of victory since the disappearance of Ayrton Senna. Now that Rubens is with the mythical Ferrari team, he has given hope to millions of his compatriots.

In Italy, they already have a soft spot for the driver who speaks their language. But then his grandfather came from the northern part of the province of Venice. He's already been adopted as a quasi-Italian. Normally, he should benefit from equal status with his prestigious teammate. Under these conditions, he can certainly be optimistic. He should certainly be a front runner. He has as much talent as anyone. He's only lacked a top flight car in the past. The one with the Prancing Horse on it should be just the job.

First car driven?
An old 'GM' when I was 6.

Your personal car?
An Alfa 166.

Favourite or dream car?
I love Ferraris.

Most memorable race car?
The Stewart SF3 in Brazil in 1999.

Sweetest racing memory?
The 1999 Brazilian Grand Prix when I was leading.

Worst racing memory?
Imola in 1994 and the Brazilian Grand Prix in 1995 when I was under too much pressure.

Your favourite circuit?
Interlagos in Brazil.

Your least favourite circuit?
None. Every track has its own character.

Which driver from the past do you admire most?
Ayrton Senna and Jackie Stewart.

Which current driver do you admire most?
None in particular.

Your favourite food?
Pasta.

Favourite drink?
Pepsi Light.

What sport do you do?
Running, squash, jet-ski, tennis and little bit of skiing since I tried it first this winter at Madonna di Campiglio.

What are your favourite sports ?
Football, jet-ski and GP motor-cycles.

Who is your favourite sportsman?
I follow the Corinthians football team in Brazil, Ayrton Senna always, and Peter Sampras.

What are your hobbies?
Bowling.

Your favourite films?
All of Robert De Niro's films, 'American Pie' and ' Sixth Sense'.

Favourite actors?
Cameron Diaz and Robert De Niro.

What do you watch on television?
Comedy shows.

What's your favourite colour?
Blue.

Favourite music?
I prefer Brazilian groups.

What do you read?
Sports papers and magazines.

What is your goal in racing?
To become World Champion.

Outside motor racing, whom do you admire?
My family.

If you had to be marooned on a desert island, who or what would you take with you?
My wife Silvana.

What do you think is the most important thing in life?
To be happy.

What is it that fascinates you about your profession?
The sensation of speed, and winning.

What don't you like about it?
The politics.

What are your best qualities?
Individuality.

What are your faults?
I'm not at my best when I'm under pressure.

Have you thought what you are going to do after Formula One?
I'm going to live in Miami...

Date of birth : May 23 1972
Place : Sao Paolo (Brazil)
Nationality : Brazilian
Residence : Monte Carlo
Marital status : Married to Silvana
Height : 1.72 m
Weight : 79 kg
Web-site :
www.barrichello.com.br

BENSON & HEDGES
JORDAN

ENGINE
Mugen-Honda MF-301 HE
Number of cylinders : 72 degree V10
Capacity : 2999 cc
Power: 810 bhp
Weight : 105 kilos

The former bank clerk from Dublin has certainly done well. While rock 'n roll remains his passion, Eddie Jordan irresistibly works his way up the Formula One ladder. Founded in 1991, Jordan Grand Prix this year celebrates its tenth anniversary having worked its way up, year by year. Last year, the team finished third in both championships.

The signing of Heinz-Harald Frentzen to this humane and family-like team was crowned with success. He regained his confidence, after suffering at Williams, and he had an exceptional season with Jordan. The arrival of Jarno Trulli is a sensible move forward and should mean that Jordan could, in theory, double their points. But can they battle with McLaren and Ferrari whose resources are virtually unlimited?

Furthermore, Jordan are slightly out on a limb in comparison to British American Racing, for they use a customer version of the Honda engine, while BAR are the Japanese giant's number one team.

Can this duplication continue to work? Jordan may not have the support of a major manufacturer but they have good sponsors and they work miracles. They move mountains, and their progress over the last ten years is a fine example of the sport.

BENSON & HEDGES JORDAN

JORDAN MUGEN-HONDA EJ 10
Tyres Bridgestone
Address : Jordan Grand Prix Ltd
Buckingham Road, Silverstone,
Northamptonshire NN12 8TJ
England
Tel : + 44 (0) 13 27 85 08 00
Fax : + 44 (0) 13 27 85 79 93
Web-site : www.jordangp.com
Team principal : Eddie Jordan
Technical director: Mike Gascoyne
Employees : 202
G.P. debut: U. S. GP 1991 (Phoenix)
G.P. participations : 146
First win : Belgium 1998 (D. Hill)
Number of wins : 3
Number of pole positions : 2
Number of points scored: 213
Best position in World Constructors' championship:
3rd in 1999
Best position in World Drivers' championship: H.H. Frentzen, 3rd in 1999
Test driver : Tomas Enge (Czechoslovakia)
1999 position: 3rd (61 points)

Eddie Jordan

Mike Gascoyne

- Shooting up
- Excellent drivers
- Good budget
- Powerful and reliable engine
- Good test programme

- Rivalry between the drivers?
- No major manufacturer support
- Relationship between Honda and
- Mugen-Honda
- Infrastructure not quite up to the standard of Ferrari and McLaren

G.P. debut : Brazil 1994 (Sauber)
Best position in World Drivers' championship : 2nd in 1997 (Williams)
96 Grand Prix participations, 142 points scored, 3 wins, 2 pole positions
-1988 German Formula Opel Lotus Champion
F1 record:
-1994 : Sauber, 7 points, 13th in championship
-1995 : Sauber, 15 points, 9th in championship
-1996 : Sauber, 7 points, 12th in championship
-1997 : Williams, 42 points, 2nd in championship
-1998 : Williams, 17 points, 7th in championship
-1999 : Jordan, 54 points, 3rd in championship

HEINZ-HARALD FRENTZEN

BENSON & HEDGES JORDAN

It might well have sunk a lesser driver. Heinz-Harald Frentzen's term at Williams was not a success, and one wondered if he could remain in Formula One. His fairy godmother came in the unlikely form of Eddie Jordan, who had run him in Formula 3000 in 1990. He decided to help him regain his confidence. It was an excellent idea. Hill was on the downward slope to retirement and Heinz-Harald gave the team some hope, and they, in turn, returned his confidence with interest, resulting in third in the championship behind the McLarens and Ferraris.

In fact he was the revelation of last season. He won twice and finished third in the Drivers' championship. This year, he remains one of the favourites, providing his car allows him to fight with the best of them. So Eddie Jordan can rely on his great talent and steely determination to continue his ascent through the hierarchy of Formula One. The presence of Jarno Trulli in the team will be supplementary motivation and will prevent Heinz-Harald from resting on his laurels.

First car driven?
An old Mercedes 280 SE when I was seven.

Your personal car?
A Mercedes SLK 230, a BMW estate, and when it comes out, I'll buy an Audi A2.

Favourite or dream car?
I haven't really got one.

Most memorable race car?
That will be the Jordan EJ 10 in year 2000.

Sweetest racing memory?
The birth of my child!

Worst racing memory?
My accident at Montreal in 1999.

Your favourite circuit?
There isn't a perfect circuit.

Your least favourite circuit?
Imola, even though I won there in 1997!

Which driver from the past do you admire most?
Senna, Prost and Mansell.

Which current driver do you admire most?
I like Alesi because he really goes for it sometimes!

Favourite food?
Paella which my mother makes for me, fish and pasta.

Favourite drink?
Apple juice and sparkling water.

What sport do you do?
Running, physical training and mountain biking which I like doing in the Spanish mountains.

What are your favourite sports?
Football, mountain biking and recreational sports.

Who is your favourite sportsman?
Christopher Columbus, it was amazing what he did all those years ago.

What are your hobbies?
I'm very keen on aviation, radio-controlled planes, mechanical things and engineering in general, and I like playing with my DVD camera.

Your favourite films?
I can't even remember the name of the last film that I saw! I'm going to spend any free time that I have with my family.

Favourite actors?
I'm not a great film fan.

What do you watch on television?
I don't watch it often.

What's your favourite colour?
Blue.

Favourite music?
U2, Simple Minds, Phil Collins and rap.

What do you read?
German newspapers.

What is your goal in racing?
To win in F1.

Outside motor racing, whom do you admire?
No one in particular.

If you had to be marooned on a desert island, who or what would you take with you?
My wife Tanja and my baby, a cook and some music.

What do you think is the most important thing in life?
Good health and to be optimistic.

What is it that fascinates you about your profession?
I've always dreamed of having an engine behind me.

What don't you like about it?
Intrigue and politics.

What are your best qualities?
Having my ideas in place.

What are your faults?
I find it difficult to change my mind.

Have you thought what you are going to do after Formula One?
No.

Date of birth : May 18 1967
Place : Monchengladbach (Germany)
Nationality : German
Residence : Monte Carlo
Marital status : Married to Tanja
Height : 1.74 m
Weight : 64.5 kg
Web-site : www.hhf.de

G.P. debut: Australia 1997 (Minardi)
Best position in World Championship : 11th in 1999 (Prost)
45 Grand Prix participations, 11 points scored, 0 wins, 0 pole positions
-1996 German F3 Champion
F1 Record:
-1997 : Minardi and Prost, 3 points, 15th in championship
-1998 : Prost, 1 point, 17th in championship
-1999 : Prost, 7 points, 11th in championship

JARNO TRULLI

BENSON & HEDGES JORDAN

Jarno Trulli is starting his fourth year in Formula One. Having driven for Minardi and Prost, the Italian driver's career is this year at a turning point. He's now in a top team which could mean that if things go right for him, he could become one of the great names of Formula One. He has the talent, the determination and the ambition to succeed.

The fact that he finds himself in the same team as Frentzen this year, will allow him to find his true position in the world of Formula One. He comes from Pescara, a small town in the south of Italy which used to host Formula One races, including a Grand Prix in 1957. Trulli has spent more than fifteen years in motor sport - karts and then Formula Three cars - before moving into Formula One. That experience stood him in good stead at Prost where last year he was perfectly poised to claim a fine second place at the Nürburgring, a testament to his loyalty and talent.

Now, at Jordan, he's with one of the best teams in the field and he'll be absorbing all that goes on around him. So how does he describe his new team owner? "With Eddie, you can only talk about playing the drums, money and women. He's very good at what he does. He does the maximum he can to get as much money as possible for his team, and to give as little of it to his drivers as possible!"

In spite of his fiercely Italian features, Jarno is already beginning to understand the character of his new team. Many people see him as a champion of the future.

First car driven?
A Renault Clio when I was 18.

Your personal car?
I still have a Peugeot 406 Coup≠ and a Fiat 500.

Favourite or dream car?
I don't have one.

Most memorable race car?
The 1996 Dallara F3 car.

Sweetest racing memory?
The first time I was on the rostrum in F1: Nurburgring in 1999.

Worst racing memory?
I prefer to forget things like that.

Your favourite circuit?
Hockenheim is my most lucky circuit; I've always done well there in F3 and in F1.

Your least favourite circuit?
Monte Carlo. It's too small for F1.

Which driver from the past do you admire most?
Niki Lauda.

Which current driver do you admire most?
No one in particular.

Your favourite food?
Pizza.

Favourite drink?
Coca-Cola.

What sport do you do?
Karting, cycling, jogging, gymnastics.

What are your favourite sports?
Alpine skiing, motorcycle Grands Prix, kart races.

Who is your favourite sportsman?
Marco Pantani, Max Biaggi.

What are your hobbies?
I'm very interested in my Trulli line of karts which are made near Venice.

Your favourite films?
Crime and comedy films.

Favourite actors?
Cameron Diaz in 'There's something about Mary'.

What do you watch on television?
I rarely watch it.

What's your favourite colour?
Red.

Favourite music?
Elton John, Vasco Rossi, rock, funk, techno and Simply Red's most recent CD.

What do you read?
I read the newspapers occasionally.

What is your goal in racing?
To get to the top.

Outside motor racing, whom do you admire?
My family.

If you had to be marooned on a desert island, who or what would you take with you?
A kart, overalls and a helmet!

What do you think is the most important thing in life?
The family and to feel good.

What is it that fascinates you about your profession?
Driving and the fact that a team can become a second family.

What don't you like about it?
The reactions of the press, sometimes. Some journalists always try to make you say something that you don't want to say.

What are your best qualities?
I don't know.

What are your faults?
I'm too much of a perfectionist.

Have you thought what you are going to do after Formula One?
No! Not yet.

Date of birth: July 13 1974
Place: Pescara (Italy)
Nationality : Italian
Residence : Francavilla (Italy) and Monte Carlo
Marital status: bachelor
Height: 1.73 m
Weight : 60 kg
Web-site: www.jarnotrulli.com

JAGUAR RACING

'The cat is back.' After a legendary career in endurance racing, Ford-owned Jaguar is back in racing again, but this time, and for the first time, in Formula One. It's an interesting confrontation with Mercedes and BMW, and a change of tack for Ford who have usually provided engines. This time, however, having bought the Stewart-Ford team, they have re-named the team Jaguar.

Actually it's not really a new team at all. While green has replaced white as the main colour, the basic team structure is the same as Stewart's. And while Jackie himself has taken a back seat, his son Paul is still there and so is nearly everyone else. Johnny Herbert remains in the team, now joined by Eddie Irvine. Unreliability struck during the winter, but the team's aim is to push Jordan out of third spot for an eventual tilt at the top two.

When it comes to the drivers, it will be interesting to see how Irvine fares now that he is no longer in Michael Schumacher's shadow. Will he be a leader of men? Herbert is sure to try and keep him honest. Formula One, meanwhile, welcomes another famous name, that of Jaguar, and so the legend continues.

ENGINE
Ford-Cosworth CR-2
Number of cylinders : 10 V 72 degree
Capacity : 2998 cc
Power : 815 bhp
Weight : 97 kilos

JAGUAR RACING

■ JAGUAR-COSWORTH-R1
Tyres Bridgestone
Address : Jaguar Racing Ltd
Bradbourne Drive
Tilbrook, Milton Keynes MK7 8BJ
England
Tel : + 44 (0) 19 08 27 97 00
Fax : + 44 (0) 19 08 279 711
Web-site : www.jaguar-racing.com
Team principal : Neil Ressler
Technical director : Gary Anderson
Employees : 250
G.P. debut: Australia 1997 (Stewart)
G.P. participations : 49 (Stewart)
Number of wins : 1 (J. Herbert)
Number of pole positions : 1 (R. Barrichello)
Number of points scored : 47 points (Stewart)
Best position in World Constructors' championship: 4th in 1999 (Stewart)
Best position in World Drivers' championship : 7th in 1999 (R. Barrichello)
Test driver : Luciano Burti (Brazil)
1999 position : 4th (36 points, Stewart)

Neil Ressler

Gary Anderson

- On the way up
- Motivation of a prestige marque
- Good budget from Ford
- Excellent engine
- 2000 car ready in December 1999
- Drivers very strong in the races

- Is Eddie Irvine a Number One driver?
- Rivalry between the drivers?
- A team which has grown too quickly

Neil Ressler, Jac Nasser and Paul Stewart hold the future of Jaguar in their hands

G.P. debut: Japan 1993 (Jordan)
Best position in World Drivers' championship : 2nd in 1999 (Ferrari)
97 Grand Prix participations, 173 points scored, 0 pole position, 4 wins
F1 record :
-1993 : Jordan, (2 G.Ps. entered), 0 point
-1994 : Jordan, 6 points, 14th in championship
-1995 : Jordan, 10 points, 12th in championship
-1996 : Ferrari, 11 points, 10th in championship
-1997 : Ferrari, 24 points, 7th in championship
-1998 : Ferrari, 47 points, 4th in championship
-1999 : Ferrari, 74 points, 2nd in championship

EDDIE IRVINE

JAGUAR RACING

■ Fresh from his four victories last year, Eddie Irvine has hit the jackpot. He may not have won the World Championship with Ferrari, but he has succeeded in something which he would almost find equally important: he's doubled his salary in becoming number one driver with Jaguar.

But he's still in a difficult situation. Without Michael Schumacher, it was obvious that he was having trouble sorting the car out for himself. So how is he going to get on this year, now that he's number one driver in the salary stakes? He's got responsibilities.

'Bad Irv', some call him, always has a girlfriend in the background and playing life to the full. They say that he prefers night-clubs and beer to sports halls. Like James Hunt 20 years ago, he likes living the life of a racing driver as much as the racing itself.

But at least he's different, very different to the majority of his colleagues who seem to come out of the same mould. He may seem arrogant, even insolent and his attitude seems rebellious, but some seem to like it. He doesn't fear anyone.

In the past, he's often proved to be very reliable during the race. But will that be enough to confirm his standing as team leader. His reputation is at stake.

First car driven?
I don't remember.

Your personal car?
A Jaguar XKR and a MKII.

Favourite or dream car?
Ferrari GTO and the Porsche 959.

Most memorable race car?
The most fun was the Toyota I drove at Le Mans in 1994. If not that, then I have a weakness for last year's Ferrari F399.

Sweetest racing memory?
My first Grand Prix win at Melbourne in 1999.

Worst racing memory?
The disappointment at Monza last year.

Your favourite circuit?
Suzuka.

Your least favourite circuit?
Silverstone.

Which driver from the past do you admire most?
Ayrton Senna.

Which current driver whom you admire most?
No one at the moment.

Your favourite food?
Sausage and peas, and Chinese food.

Favourite drink?
Miller beer.

What sport do you do?
Golf, jogging, snowboard, swimming and cycling.

What are your favourite sports?
Golf, sailing and cycling.

Who is your favourite sportsman?
I like golfers, certain cyclists and the motorcycle racer Valentino Rossi.

What are your hobbies?
Snowboarding, fishing, sailing and travelling. I like to be on the move. Hours in a plane don't worry me.

Your favourite films?
Amusing films.

Favourite actors?
The actress Liam Neesen.

What do you watch on television?
Films, documentaries and sports programmes.

What's your favourite colour?
Blue.

Favourite music?
Rock in general, Van Morrison, AC/DC, Cranberries, U2 and Oasis.

What do you read?
I don't like reading.

What's your goal in racing?
Always to find a drive with a top team.

Outside motor racing, whom do you admire?
Bob Geldof for his Live Aid foundation.

If you had to be marooned on a desert island, who or what would you take with you?
A very beautiful girl.

What do you think is the most important thing in life?
To have fun and to feel good.

What is it that fascinates you about your profession?
Being a star.

What don't you like about it?
Danger is never far away.

What are your best qualities?
I've too many!

What are your faults?
I haven't any.

Have you thought what you are going to do after Formula One?
Go fishing.

Date of birth : November 10 1965
Place: Newtownards (Northern Ireland)
Nationality : Irish
Residence : Dublin (Ireland) and Milan (Italy)
Marital status : bachelor
Height: 1.78 m
Weight : 70 kg
Web-site : www.eddie-irvine.com

G.P. debut: Brazil 1989 (Benetton)
Best position in World Drivers' championship : 4th in 1995 (Benetton)
144 Grand Prix participations, 98 points scored, 3 wins , 0 pole position
-1987 British F3 Champion
-1991 Winner Le Mans (Mazda)
F1 record:
-1989 : Benetton and Tyrrell, (6 G.Ps. entered), 5 points, 14th in championship
-1990 : Lotus, (2 G.Ps. entered), 0 point
-1991 : Lotus, (7 G.Ps. entered), 0 point
-1992 : Lotus, 2 points, 14th in championship
-1993 : Lotus, 11 points, 8th in championship
-1994 : Lotus, Ligier and Benetton, 0 point
-1995 : Benetton, 45 points, 4th in championship
-1996 : Sauber, 4 points, 14th in championship
-1997 : Sauber, 15 points, 10th in championship
-1998 : Sauber, 1 point, 15th in championship
-1999 : Stewart, 15 points, 8th in championship

JOHNNY HERBERT

JAGUAR RACING

We all love Johnny, the clown prince of Formula One, who will always lighten the atmosphere at a Grand Prix. He did, of course, suffer for his art. In spite of badly breaking both legs in a Formula 3000 accident at Brands Hatch in 1988, he made his debut with Benetton the next year, walking on crutches. But he's still with us, the most experienced driver, with Alesi, in the field. He's a typical British driver: a fighter, gritty but there at the end.

So this is his 12th season of Formula One in which he has won three Grands Prix, scored nearly 100 points, and also won Le Mans in 1991. He's not great at qualifying, but he's formidable in the race itself. He may not have done much at Sauber for three years, but Jackie Stewart gave him the chance to re-launch his career last year.

And after a heap of bad luck, he took his chance when it came, watching leader after leader retire at Nurburgring, to hang on in there and win, writing the Stewart name in the record books before the team changed itsname to Jaguar.

"Johnny be good" sang Chuck Berry, much of which is lost on Johnny although he's certainly still good on the track. So teammate Eddie Irvine might be ahead of him on the grids, but will it be the same at the flag? That's not so certain.

He may not be taken seriously, but he still has a lot to offer. He needs to shake off the unlucky tag, but the prospect of a new team and an old adversary as his teammate will give him new motivation.

First car driven?
An Austin Mini when I was about 10.

Your personal car?
A Jaguar XKR Coupe.

Favourite or dream car?
An Aston Martin DB7.

Most memorable race car?
The 1992 Lotus.

Sweetest racing memory?
My win at Nurburgring in 1999 with Stewart.

Worst racing memory?
My accident at Brands Hatch in 1988 in F3000.

Your favourite circuit?
Spa, it's fabulous.

Your least favourite circuit?
Hockenheim and Fuji.

Which driver from the past do you admire most?
Gilles Villeneuve.

Which current driver do you admire most?
No one in particular.

Your favourite food?
Pasta.

Favourite drink?
Sparkling water.

What sport do you do?
Golf, physical training and cycling.

What are your favourite sports?
Golf.

Who is your favourite sportsman?
The decathlete Daly Thomson.

What are your hobbies?
Golf, swimming and computer science. I've just built one and it works!

Your favourite films?
Action films: 'Braveheart', 'American Pie' and 'There's something about Mary'.

Favourite actors?
Mel Gibson, Buster Keaton and Sandra Bullock.

What do you watch on television?
The news and comedy.

What's your favourite colour?
The colours of my helmet.

Favourite music?
Chris Rea, Eric Clapton, Eagles, Aerosmith and Black Sabbath.

What do you read?
Books and magazines on the technicalities of sport.

What is your goal in racing?
To be World Champion.

Outside motor racing, whom do you admire most?
The great humanitarian causes.

If you had to be marooned on a desert island, who or what would you take with you?
The most beautiful girl in the world.

What do you think is the most important thing in life?
My family and to be happy.

What is it that fascinates you about your profession?
The sensation of speed and the satisfaction of a qualifying lap.

What don't you like about it?
I love it all.

What are your best qualities?
It's not up to me to say.

What are your faults?
I'm too laid-back.

Have you thought what you are going to do after Formula One?
No not yet.

Date of birth : June 27 1964
Place : Romford (England)
Nationality : British
Residence : Monte Carlo
Marital status: : Married to Rebecca, with two girls, Amy and Chloe
Web-site : www.johnnyherbert.co.uk

BMW.WILLIAMS F1

This team is on the crest of a wave. Worried by the vulnerability of his business, Frank Williams succumbed to the general tendency by tying up with BMW. Following Renault's departure, the team with a remarkable record of wins and titles was slowly sliding downhill. In spite of the talent of Ralf Schumacher who succeeded in damage limitation, a quick fix was needed to halt the slide. The arrival of the Munich manufacturer was a heaven-sent opportunity.

It was thought that this year would be one of transition and learning. But at Melbourne, the reliability of the BMW engine surprised many, and Ralf Schumacher hung on in there for third place. While it was reliable in one car, it was less so in the other, where young Jenson Button acquitted himself well, even if he didn't get to the end. Certainly, the Williams pair attracted the right kind of publicity, especially as they constitute the youngest team in the paddock at 44 years in total - and they could just shine in the new colours of BMW-Williams.

ENGINE
BMW V 10
Number of cylinders: 72 degree V10
Capacity : 2998 cc
Power : 800 bhp
Weight : 120 kilos

BMW.WILLIAMS F I

■ **WILLIAMS F1 BMW FW 22**
Tyres Bridgestone
Address : Williams F1, Grove, Wantage,
Oxfordshire, OX12 0DQ
England.
Tel : + 44 (0) 12 35 77 77 00
Fax : + 44 (0) 12 35 76 47 05
Web-site : www.williamsf1.co.uk
Team Principal : Frank Williams
Technical director : Patrick Head
Employees : 360
G.P. debut : Argentina 1978
G.P. participations: 411
First win : British 1979 (C. Regazzoni)
Number of wins : 103
Number of pole positions : 108
Number of points scored : 1982.5
World Constructors' titles : 9 (1980, 81, 86, 87, 92, 93, 94, 96 and 97)
World Drivers' titles: 7 (Jones 1980, Rosberg 1982, Piquet 1986,
Mansell 1992, Prost 1993, D. Hill 1996, J. Villeneuve 1997)
Test driver : Bruno Junqueira (Brazil)
1999 position: 5th (35 points)

Frank Williams

Patrick Head

- Partnership and budget from BMW	- Very young drivers
- Good technical team	- Jenson Button's inexperience
- An experienced team	- Reliability of BMW engine?
- Ralf Schumacher	
- Desire to get back on top	

BMW.WilliamsF1Team

9

G.P. debut: Australia 1997 (Jordan)
Best position in World Championship: 6th in 1999 (Williams)
49 Grand Prix participations, 62 points scored, 0 wins, 0 pole position
-1995 Winner of Macau F3
-1996 Japanese F3000 Champion
F1 record:
-1997 : Jordan, 13 points, 11th in championship
-1998 : Jordan, 14 points, 10th in championship
-1999 : Williams, 35 points, 6th in championship

RALF SCHUMACHER

BMW.WILLIAMS F1

When young Ralf Schumacher made his debut with Jordan back in 1997, he had all the characteristic traits of a spoilt brat. He was typically temperamental and inaccessible. To say that he was bigheaded wasn't describing his hat size. He was proud of his name, although he hadn't established his own first name. And to be truthful, the initial results weren't fantastic either. Teammate Fisichella had the measure of his pretentious teammate.

The following year, the arrival of Damon Hill made him more humble. The kid matured. And when he went to Williams in 1999, the transformation was nearly complete. The younger Schumacher had changed.

Driving in a team where human values aren't essential, Schumi Junior scored excellent results at a difficult time. He saved the team from disaster.

Zanardi never had a chance. The young German was the revelation of the season. He became part of the Formula One establishment.

The moody young man of Formula One has become smiling, approachable, reasonable. This year, BMW's challenge makes the season character building.

But on last year's showing, he should be up to it. He wasn't overly ambitious and declared modestly: "it would be unrealistic to think about a rostrum position this season. We must finish races and score points from time to time."

First car driven?
A Fiat 500 when I was seven.

Your personal car?
A BMW M5.

Favourite or dream car?
Nothing currently.

Most memorable race car?
The 1999 Williams FW 21 and the 1998 Jordan.

Sweetest racing memory?
Monza 1998 - in fact all the rostrums I shared with my brother but also Monza in 1999.

Worst racing memory?
Last year, I was leading at Nurburgring when I suffered a puncture. What should have been my best racing memory instead became the worst.

Your favourite circuit?
Monaco.

Your least favourite circuit?
None in particular.

Which driver from the past do you admire most?
No one really.

Which current driver do you admire most?
My brother Michael of course.

Your favourite food?
Pasta.

Favourite drink?
Apple juice with sparkling water.

What sport do you do?
Physical training, karting and tennis.

What are your favourite sports?
Basketball, athletics and the Olympics.

Who is your favourite sportsman?
In general, all the top sportsmen.

What are your hobbies?
To go out on my boat, do some jet skiing, play backgammon. I'm also studying for my pilot's licence.

Your favourite films?
Actions films. I liked 'The world is not enough' the most recent James Bond.

Favourite actors?
Bill Cosby.

What do you watch on television?
Nothing in particular. Television is a distraction.

What's your favourite colour?
Dark colours.

Favourite music?
'Soft' rock.

What do you read?
I don't like reading much.

What is your goal in racing?
I have a long term contract with Williams. The challenge is with BMW and it's demanding.

Outside motor racing, whom do you admire most?
My brother and my family.

If you had to be marooned on a desert island, who or what would you takewith you?
A boat to leave in as soon as possible.

What do you think is the most important thing in life?
First of all, it is health, but also to win in life and succeed in achieving the goals that one has set oneself.

What is it that fascinates you about your profession?
Principally, it's the driving.

What don't you like about it?
I love racing too much.

What are your best qualities?
I'm very strong mentally.

What are your faults?
I'm too egotistical!

Have you thought what you are going to do after Formula One?
Without doubt, return to Kerpen and race karts against my brother.

Date of birth: June 30 1975
Place: Huerth (Germany)
Nationality : German
Residence : Monte Carlo
Marital status : bachelor
Height : 1.78 m
Weight : 73 kg
Web-site : www.ralf-schumacher.net

G.P. debut: Australia 2000 (Williams)
-1998 British Formula Ford Champion

JENSON BUTTON

BMW.WILLIAMS F1

The very least you can say about the arrival of Jenson Button in Formula One is that it's caused a lot of ink to flow. In England, no one is talking about anything else than this kid of 20 who is only in his third year of motor racing - and in Formula One - after an apprenticeship in karts.

All the pundits have been consulted to give their word of advice on the wisdom of giving young Jenson a Formula One drive.

Williams is on the crest of a wave with its new partner BMW. This new partnership isn't a symbol of safety and reliability in the short term. How would the relatively inexperienced young Briton react to this new environment? Was it not a poisoned chalice to enter into the big time with so little technical experience?

The team's directors have been unanimous in their praise for Jenson's undisputed talent and consider him a phenomenon. But will they still be saying the same thing if this year of apprenticeship isn't a success?

The boy himself seems happy enough, insensitive to the pressure and utterly calm.

First car driven?
An Audi on the runway of a disused airfield when I was eight.

Your personal car?
A BMW M5 and a Ferrari F355

Favourite or dream car?
The BMW M5 was a dream; a Lotus Esprit or a TVR Siberia.

Most memorable race car?
It can only be a Formula One car, a Williams...

Sweetest racing memory?
The European Super A kart championship in 1997, and my second place in Macau in 1999.

Worst racing memory?
I finished second in the Super A kart championship, just a couple of seconds behind the winner.

Your favourite circuit?
The Grand Prix circuit at Silverstone.

Your least favourite circuit?
Croix en Ternois in the north of France.

Which driver from the past do you admire most?
The Ayrton Senna and Alain Prost era, and Michael Schumacher.

Which current driver do you admire most?
Michael Schumacher. But I'm going to try and make it me.

Your favourite food?
Pasta.

Favourite drink?
Orange juice.

What sport do you do?
Gymnastics, body boarding, cycling and mountain biking, surfing and swimming.

What are your favourite sports?
Downhill alpine skiing, European Cup football matches and the World Cup, and mountain bike races.

Who is your favourite sportsman?
Liverpool football player Michael Owen and the skier Alberto Tomba.

What are your hobbies?
Surfing the internet, shopping and having fun with my friends.

Your favourite films?
'Cruel Intention'.

Favourite actors?
I prefer actresses like Julia Roberts in 'Pretty Woman' and 'Notting Hill'.

What do you watch on television?
I don't like television.

What's your favourite colour?
Blue and white which just happen to be BMW's colours.

Favourite music?
DJ dance music, techno and disco.

What do you read?
Motor racing magazines.

What is your goal in racing?
To be World Champion.

Outside motor racing, whom do you admire?
The singer Britney Spears.

If you had to be marooned on a desert island, who or what would you take with you?
A boat, my girlfriend Kimberley and a motor racing magazine.

What do you think is the most important thing in life?
Health and good humour.

What is it that fascinates you about your profession?
The sensation of speed, competition and the life of a team.

What don't you like about it?
There's too much I like about it.

What are your best qualities?
I'm relaxed and I don't like criticising others.

What are your faults?
I like winning too much.

Have you thought what you are going to do after Formula One?
I would like to remain in motor sport. But I'm still only 20

Jenson and his father, John, his twentieth birthday.

Date of birth : January 19 1980
Place : Frome (England)
Nationality: British
Residence : Bicester (England)
Marital status: girlfriend Kimberley
Height : 1.81 m
Weight : 74 kg
Web-site : www.jensonbutton.com

MILD SEVEN BENETTON PLAYLIFE

Since Michael Schumacher left them at the end of 1995, the Benetton team's results have nose-dived. Despite several changes of management and a constant flow of new technical staff, there seemed to be no stopping the decline. It was time for a major change and that was announced just days after the Australian Grand Prix. Weary with the effort, the Benetton family as good as admitted it could not keep up with the pace of the sport and the huge budgets required in Formula 1. It announced it had sold the outfit to Renault for 120 million dollars, but would continue to sponsor the team to the end of 2001.

The French car company, with six world championships to its name, would once again hit the grand prix trail with its own team, as from 2002. It appointed Flavio Briatore to take control of the team which he had led to glory in the Schumi days. Briatore would thus leave Supertec to oversee the handing over of power from the Anglo-Italian team to Renault. Fisichella and Wurz are to be kept on as the drivers.

Their mission is clear: to inject some colour back into the team and push Benetton and Supertec back to the front of the grid, once Renault takes over the reins.

ENGINE
Supertec Playlife FB 02
Number of cylinders: 71 degree V10
Capacity : 2999 cc
Power : 780 bhp
Weight : 117 kilos

MILD SEVEN BENETTON PLAYLIFE

MILD SEVEN BENETTON PLAYLIFE B 200
Tyres Bridgestone
Address : Benetton Formula Ltd
Whiteways Technical Center, Enstone,
Chipping, Norton, Oxfordshire OX7 4EE
England.
Tel : + 44 (0) 16 08 67 80 00
Fax : + 44 (0) 16 08 67 86 09
Web-site : www.benettonf1.com
Team principal : Rocco Benetton
Technical director : Pat Symonds
Employees : 320
G.P. debut: Italy 1981 (Toleman) and Brazil 1986 (Benetton)
G.P. participations : 283
First win : Mexico 1986 (G. Berger)
Number of wins : 27
Number of pole positions : 16
Number of points scored : 846.5
World Constructors' titles : 1 (1995)
World Drivers' titles : 2 (M. Schumacher in 1994 and 1995)
Test driver : Hidetoshi Mitsusada (Japan)
1999 position: 6th (16 points)

Flavio Briatore

Pat Symonds

- New Supertec engine
- Good drivers
- Well tried car
- Desire to get back on top
- Good enough budget
- Bought by Renault for 2001

- Supertec engine potential?
- Very young boss (30 years old)
- On a downward spiral

G.P. debut: Australia 1996 (Minardi)
Best position in World Drivers' Championship : 8th
57 Grand Prix participations, 49 points scored, 0 wins, 1 pole position
-1994 Italian F3 Champion
-1994 Winner Monaco Grand Prix F3 race
F1 record:
-1996 : Minardi, (8 G.Ps. entered), 0 point
-1997 : Jordan, 20 points, 8th in championship
-1998 : Benetton, 16 points, 9th in championship
-1999 : Benetton, 13 points, 9th in championship

GIANCARLO FISICHELLA

MILD SEVEN BENETTON PLAYLIFE

■ In 1999, 'Fisico' held onto the ninth place where he'd finished the year before. But this season hadn't been as spectacular. His Benetton was certainly less competitive and contributed to this drop in performance.

If Giancarlo Fisichella wants to continue his climb to the top, then he can't be satisfied with these average results. He is confident in his team to redress the balance.

He's about to tackle his third season with a team that has lost much of its prestige. He can't wait much longer. Last year, he was about to win his first Grand Prix, at the Nurburgring, when his car got away from him on the wet tarmac.

The year 2000 is an important one for him. If he wants to bounce back, then the 27-year old has all the talent if his Benetton B200 is the car in which to do it.

First car driven?
A Fiat 127 when I was four or five.

Your personal car?
Mercedes CL Coupe 5500 AMG.

Favourite or dream car?
It was the 996 version of the Porsche 911. Now I'm going to have the bi-turbo.

Most memorable race car?
My Formula One cars.

Sweetest racing memory?
Formula Three at Monte Carlo in 1994, Spa with Jordan in 1997 and Canada with Benetton in 1998.

Worst racing memory?
When I retired while I was leading at Nurburgring last year.

Your favourite circuit?
Imola.

Your least favourite circuit?
I don't have one.

Which driver from the past do you admire most?
Ayrton Senna.

Which current driver do you admire most?
Michael Schumacher, Villeneuve and Hakkinen.

Favourite food?
Les Bucatini alla matriciana which is pasta in Roman style.

Favourite drink?
Coca cola and orange juice.

What sport do you do?
Football, tennis, skiing, jogging, mountain biking and gymnastics.

What are your favourite sports?
I like all sports and football more than anything.

Who is your favourite sportsman?
The footballers Francesco Totti of AC Roma and Sinisa Mihaljovic of Lazio, Rome who are friends of mine.

What are your hobbies?
I am a big fan of the football club AC Roma. I also like music, fishing and being with my friends.

Your favourite films?
Comedy films and 'It's a Wonderful Life'.

Favourite actors?
Sylvester Stallone, Sharon Stone and Roberto Benigni.

What do you watch on television?
A bit of everything.

What's your favourite colour?
Blue.

Favourite music?
Elton John, Claudio Baglioni and Renato Zero.

What do you read?
Motor racing magazines.

What is your goal in racing?
To be World Champion.

Outside motor racing, whom do you admire?
Cindy Crawford!

If you had to be marooned on a desert island, who or what would you take with you?
My girlfriend Luna and our daughter Carlotta.

What do you think is the most important thing in life?
Good health and a happy family life.

What is it that fascinates you about your profession?
I feel great when I'm behind a steering wheel.

What don't you like about it?
To find myself without a drive, like at the end of 1996.

What are your best qualities?
I'm kind.

What are your faults?
I'm not tough enough!

Have you thought what you are going to do after Formula One?
I'd like to stay in motor sport.

Date of birth : January 14 1973
Place : Rome (Italy)
Nationality: Italian
Residence : Rome and Monte Carlo
Marital status : married to Luna, one daughter Carlotta
Height : 1.72 m
Weight : 69 kg
Web-site : www.fisico.com

G.P. debut: Canada 1997
Best position in World Drivers' Championship : 8th in 1998 (Benetton)
-1986 Off-road World Cycling Champion
-1993 Austrian F3 Champion
-1996 Winner Le Mans 24 hours (Porsche)
35 Grand Prix participations, 24 points scored, 0 wins, 0 pole position
F1 record:
-1997 : Benetton, (3 G.Ps. entered), 4 points, 14th in championship
-1998 : Benetton, 17 points, 8th in championship
-1999 : Benetton, 3 points, 13th in championship

ALEXANDER WURZ

MILD SEVEN BENETTON PLAYLIFE

Alexander Wurz's Formula One career got off to a rapid start in 1997. He was called in to replace compatriot Gerhard Berger during the season, and finished on the rostrum in England in only his third Grand Prix.

Still with the same team, he had a much less promising season last year.

His only points-scoring result was a modest fifth place at home in Austria. Certainly, the fact that his machinery wasn't competitive had more than a little to do with his slide down the hierarchy, but it is worrying and alarming was that teammate Fisichella was less affected.

So this tall, sensible chap with one blue shoe and one red is slightly at the crossroads of his career. He needs results this year to stay in Formula One.

He's a friendly, smiling chap, always approachable, a man who loves the countryside. He needs a good year and will be counting on his car to give him a better chance. The talent that he has already shown hasn't disappeared, it's there somewhere, waiting for the right moment.

This year, Jenson Button is among his rivals. In the seventies, their fathers drove against one another in rallycross. The rivalry continues, thirty years later, on the asphalt of Grand Prix circuits.

First car driven?
A VW Beetle in an Austrian forest when I was eight.

Your personal car?
A two-seater Renault Kangoo in which I can put my mountain bike or my jet ski and a Renault Laguna V6.

Favourite or dream car?
That would be a car that didn't use petrol and which you didn't need to fill up.

Most memorable race car?
My 1992 Formula Ford Van Diemen and the Porsche at Le Mans in 1996.

Sweetest racing memory?
My win at Le Mans in 1994.

Worst racing memory?
A Vauxhall Lotus race in 1992 in Austria where I was hot favourite, but engine problems meant I had no chance.

Your favourite circuit?
Spa, Laguna Seca and the old Nurburgring.

Your least favourite circuit?
I don't like tracks which are laid out on old airports like Diepholz.

Which driver from the past do you admire most?
No one in particular.

Which current driver do you admire most?
None!

Your favourite food?
Italian cooking and pasta in particular.

Favourite drink?
Apple juice with sparkling water.

What sport do you do?
All kinds of cycling, skiing, snowboarding and squash.

What are you favourite sports?
Ice hockey, football and tennis.

Who is your favourite sportsman?
Carl Lewis.

What are your hobbies?
I love the country, mountains and climbing, of which I do a little.

Your favourite films?
Recent films like 'Ronin' with Robert de Niro and the fantastic car chase on the winding roads near La Turbie next to Monaco

Favourite actors?
Robert de Niro, Val Kilmer, Clint Eastwood and Madonna.

What do you watch on television?
'Star Trek', sports, advertisements and certain films.

What's your favourite colour?
The colours on my helmet and principally blue.

Favourite music?
The Beatles, Pink Floyd, the Stones but generally speaking, I like all types of music from classical to hard rock.

What do you read?
Political and news magazines and certain novels.

What is your goal in racing?
To keep driving as well as I can.

Outside motor racing, whom do you admire?
I haven't thought about it.

If you had to be marooned on a desert island, who or what would you take with you?
My girlfriend Karin, a knife and some water.

What do you think is the most important thing in life?
Health and happiness.

What is it that fascinates you about your profession?
Driving at the limit.

What don't you like about it?
Not having enough spare time.

What are your best qualities?
I'm relaxed.

What are your faults?
That's hard to say.

Have you thought what you are going to do after Formula One?
In this job, you meet a huge number of people, and there's no doubt that it's an excellent way of getting into business.

Date of birth : February 15 1975
Place : Waidhofen-Thaya (Austria)
Nationality : Austrian
Residence : Monte Carlo
Marital status : girlfriend Karin
Height : 1.87 m
Weight : 74 kg
Web-site : www.wurz.com

ENGINE
Peugeot A 20
Number of cylinders : 10 V 72 degree
Capacity : 2998 cm
Power : 785 bhp
Weight : 109 kilos

The Prost Grand Prix team is finding it hard to get going. The Prost-Peugeot marriage is weighed down, and like all couples close to divorce, the partners are each blaming one another, retribution flying to and fro. So at the start of the 2000 season, the atmosphere is heavy, not good.
The Prost AP 03 is entirely new, composed of some three thousand new parts.
But ever since it first turned a wheel in testing, it has suffered countless small problems. The arrival of Jean Alesi, assisted by the talented and determined Nick Heidfeld hasn't changed anything really. The French team turned up at Melbourne with a car which suffered problems which could hopefully be attributed to its lack of testing. The Peugeot engine isn't bad, the technical staff talented, and backed up by the charismatic four time World Champion, mechanics with an excellent reputation, and a sufficient budget. In brief, the Prost Grand Prix team has everything going for it. The gap between Prost and its adversaries at the start of the season is big, but not insurmountable.

GAULOISES PROST PEUGEOT

PROST-PEUGEOT Prost AP 03
Tyres Bridgestone
Address : Prost Grand Prix, Quartier des sangliers,
7, av. Eugene Freyssinet
78286 Guyancourt Cedex, France
Tel : + 33 (0) 1 39 30 11 00
Fax : + 33 (0) 1 3930 11 01
Web-site : www.prostgp.com
Team principal : Alain Prost
Technical director : Alan Jenkins
Employees : 250
G.P. debut: Ligier (Brazil 1976)
          Prost (Australia 1997)
G.P. participations : Ligier (326)
                 Prost (49)
First win : Sweden 1977 (J. Laffite)
Number of wins : 9 (Ligier)
Number of pole positions : 9 (Ligier)
Number of points scored : 389 (Ligier)
                            31 (Prost)
Best position in World Constructors' Championship:
2nd in 1980 (Ligier), 6th in 1997 (Prost)
Best position in World Drivers' championship :
J. Laffite, 2nd in 1979, 1980 and 1981 (Ligier) and
O. Panis
9th in 1997 (Prost)
Test driver : Stephane Sarrazin (France) also entered in F3000 (West
Competition)
1999 position: 7th (9 points)

Alain Prost

Alan Jenkins

+	-
- Very good technical team	- Completely new car
- Good drivers	- Peugeot engine potential
- Adequate budget	- Difficult relationship between
- Completely new car	Prost and Peugeot
	- Winter testing upset by technical problems
	- Nick Heidfeld's lack of experience

GP debut: France 1989 (Tyrrell)
Best position in World Drivers' championship: 4th in 1996 and 1997 (Benetton)
167 Grand Prix participations, 236 points scored, 1 win, 2 pole positions
-1987 French F3 Champion
-1989 Intercontinental F3000 Champion
F1 record:
-1989 : Tyrrell, (8 G.Ps. entered), 8 points, 9th in championship
-1990 : Tyrrell, 13 points, 9th in championship
-1991 : Ferrari, 21 points, 7th in championship
-1992 : Ferrari, 18 points, 7th in championship
-1993 : Ferrari, 16 points, 6th in championship
-1994 : Ferrari, 24 points, 5th in championship
-1995 : Ferrari, 42 points, 5th in championship
-1996 : Benetton, 47 points, 4th in championship
-1997 : Benetton, 36 points, 4th in championship
-1998 : Sauber, 9 points, 11th in championship
-1999 : Sauber, 2 points, 16th in championship

JEAN ALESI

GAULOISES PROST PEUGEOT

The doyen of the current drivers is still going strong. He has the energy of a debutant as he tackles his first year with his friend Alain Prost. They were teammates at Ferrari in 1991, and know one another well. Jean Alesi dreamed of the day when he would drive for Prost.

Now it's a reality. And following Olivier Panis's new career path, it means that Jean is the only Frenchman in the field. Driving for the only French team means that he is the focus of attention for his entire country. For him, it's the most exciting challenge of his entire, long career.

Often unlucky, he still doesn't have the record he deserves. His style of driving is legendary. His aggression, his flair, his ease of overtaking, of giving his utmost and his speed make him one of the most popular personalities in Formula One.

As he begins his 12th season at the peak of motor sport, he still has a passion for racing that even some newcomers don't have. If the Prost AP 03 is competitive, if the Peugeot engine satisfies the hopes of the whole team, Jean Alesi will look after everything else. But if that's not the case, one can still count on 'Jean d'Avignon' when the weather comes out of the hills. In such conditions, he's fantastic. In fact, one almost hopes for rain because it's so good to watch Jean in those conditions.

First car driven?
I was less than 10 years old and it was a Fiat 850. I must have been doing 80 kph in reverse and I hit another car!

Your personal car?
A Ferrari Maranello and I still have a Fiat 500!

Favourite or dream car?
Nothing at the moment.

Most memorable race car?
The 1987 F3 Dallara and the 1989 Tyrrell 018 which was fantastic.

Sweetest racing memory?
Phoenix 1990 and my battle with Senna.

Worst racing memory?
Imola in 1994.

Your favourite circuit?
Monza for its configuration≠ and Monaco for the atmosphere.

Your least favourite circuit?
Budapest.

Which driver from the past do you admire most?
Elio de Angelis and Alain Prost.

Which current driver do you admire most?
No one in particular.

Your favourite food?
Pasta.

Favourite drink?
Sparkling water.

What sport do you do?
Weight training, cross-country skiing, jogging, cycling and climbing.

What are your favourite sports?
Football and particularly Juventus from Turin, and Alpine and slalom skiing.

Who is your favourite sportsman?
The footballers Alessandro Del Piero and Zinedine Zidane of Juventus and Alberto Tomba during his career.

What are your hobbies?
I'm very keen on my vineyard 'Clos l'Hermitage' de Lirac which is a 'Cotes du Rhone' from the Gard region.

Your favourite films?
Comedy and action films.

Favourite actors?
Robert de Niro, Sophie Marceau and Kumiko!

What do you watch on television?
Sports, the news and some documentaries.

What's your favourite colour?
Blue.

Favourite music?
Madonna and U2.

What do you read?
Books on watches and antiques.

What is your goal in racing?
To enjoy it.

Outside motor racing, whom do you admire?
Winston Churchill and the great politicians of the second World War.

If you had to be marooned on a desert island, who or what would you take with you?
A pistol in order to blow my brains out.

What do you think is the most important thing in life?
The family and health.

What is it that fascinates you about your profession?
The sensation of speed.

What don't you like about it?
I like everything.

What are your best qualities?
Frankness and speed of analysis.

What are your faults?
My frankness isn't always welcome.

Have you thought what you are going to do after Formula One?
There will always be my vines, of course, but I would like to do something with cars as well.

Date of birth : June 11 1964
Place : Avignon (France)
Nationality : French
Residence: Geneva (Switzerland)
Marital status : married to Kumiko, two daughters, Charlotte and Helena
Height : 1.70 m
Weight : 70 kg
Web-site : www.jeanalesi.com

15

Grand Prix debut with Prost (Australia 2000)
-1994 German 1600 Formula Ford champion
-1995 German 1800 Formula Ford champion
-1997 German F3 Champion
-1997 Winner of F3 Monaco Grand Prix and Macau
-1999 International F3000 champion

NICK HEIDFELD

GAULOISES PROST PEUGEOT

Nick Heidfeld is the reigning International F3000 champion, a graduate of the Mercedes talent school. At 19, he was already test driver for McLaren!

He'd covered 10,000 kilometres of testing before moving to Prost. He'd won the championship in every discipline in which he'd raced before moving into Formula One.

Some drivers look like racing drivers, but you'd never guess Nick's profession if you didn't know it. He has the look and physique of a kid still at school or college.

In spite of his age, his professionalism and his maturity are astounding. Unassuming, almost to the extent of being shy, he shows cold determination, he knows what he wants. Right from the moment he first drove for Prost, his speed and consistency impressed his new team, as much as his technical analysis.

Coming from the Mercedes school like Michael Schumacher and Heinz-Harald Frentzen amongst others, the young German driver has proved to have the motivation and talent to follow in the footsteps of his predecessors.

Of the three newcomers to Formula One this year, one can place Mazzacane to one side because of a lack of reference. But it will be fascinating to follow the careers of Nick Heidfeld and Jenson Button. Who will win the 'rookie' award?

Without wishing to pre-judge the Englishman's competence, the German appears well prepared and well armed to succeed in the battle.

First car driven?
It was on my father's knee, in one of the parking areas at the Nurburgring. I wasn't yet 10. However, I can't remember what kind of car it was.

Your personal car?
A Peugeot 406 Coupe.

Favourite or dream car?
I like a lot of cars, but I don't dream about them.

Most memorable race car?
The 1997 F3 Dallara.

Sweetest racing memory?
During one of my first tests with McLaren, at Monza in 1997, I had a small excursion off the track. After I got back to the pits, the mechanics very solemnly presented with a small bag containing all the gravel the car had picked up from the gravel trap.

Worst racing memory?
An accident at the first corner of the Formula Ford Festival at Brands Hatch in 1994.

Your favourite circuit?
Street circuits like Macau or Monaco, and the Nurburgring.

Your least favourite circuit?
Airport circuits, and Spa.

Which driver from the past do you admire most?
The battles between Prost and Senna.

Which current driver do you admire most?
None in particular.

Favourite food?
Italian food and those that are made up of lots of little different but immaculately prepared dishes

Favourite drink?
Orange juice.

What sport do you do?
Physical training, cycling and surfing.

What are your favourite sports?
I like all sports, but I don't have enough time to do them. I would like to play more tennis and golf.

Who is your favourite sportsman?
Basketball player Michael Jordan.

What are your hobbies?
Nothing special. I like to be able to relax, and go out with my girlfriend Patricia, and go to the cinema.

Your favourite films?
I love '5th Element'.

Favourite actors?
Cameron Diaz in 'There's something about Mary'.

What do you watch on television?
Motor sports and the big football and boxing matches.

What's your favourite colour?
It's between sky blue and turquoise, like the sea in the tropics.

Favourite music?
The Fugees and hits like 'No Limit' by Alliance Ethnic and 'Tomber la chemise' by Zebda.

What do you read?
I read whatever there is about motor racing.

What is your goal in racing?
To be happy in what I like doing. For the moment, that's racing, but it might be something else later in life.

Outside motor racing, whom do you admire?
No one in particular.

If you had to be marooned on a desert island, who or what would you take with you?
My girlfriend Patricia, thousands of tins of Coca-Cola and an inventor who could get us out of this mess.

What do you think is the most important thing in life?
To be happy.

What is it that fascinates you about your profession?
Driving.

What don't you like about it?
Nothing special. I haven't yet seen the bad side of the job.

What are your best qualities?
I'm a realist and I think I analyse things well.

What are your faults?
You'll see them soon.

Have you thought what you're going to do after Formula One?
No, not yet.

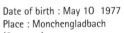

Date of birth : May 10 1977
Place : Monchengladbach (Germany)
Nationality : German
Residence : Monte Carlo
Marital status : girlfriend Patricia
Height : 1.65 m
Weight : 60 kg

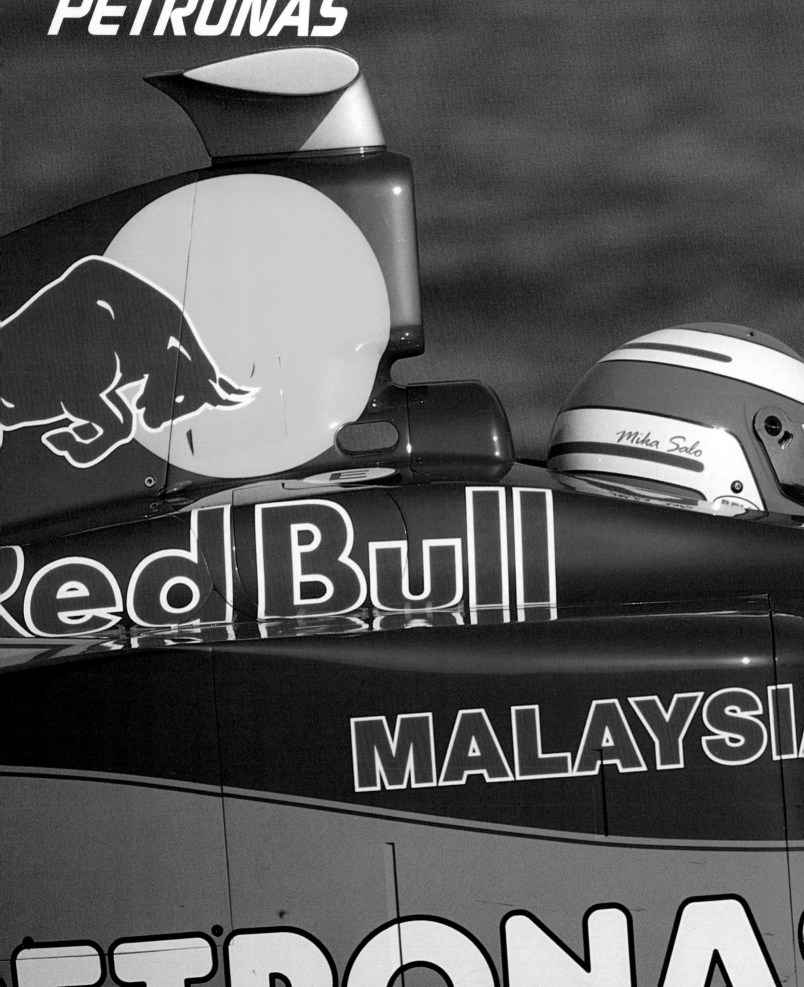

RED BULL SAUBER PETRONAS

fkg.com

This year the Sauber team, all alone in deepest Switzerland, decided to give itself a better chance of success. Last year, it was burdened by constant problems with a rear end of the car which was too heavy. So the technical department has been strengthened. The Sauber C19 for the year 2000 was ready very early on and has since covered some 5000 kilometres of testing this winter. It is reliable and competitive. Still equipped with last year's Ferrari engine which was so reliable, the team often counts on early races to allow them to score points at the expense of less reliable rivals. Mika Salo, whom the Scuderia placed with the team, achieved his aim by finishing sixth at Melbourne before being disqualified because the front wing was too wide by 20 millimetres.

The Swiss team has frequently been let down by the pace of its development. Often they've been competitive at the start of the season, but have proved incapable of developing the car in the right direction and have slipped back. The arrived of new blood in the team, and the motivation of drivers Diniz and Salo should reverse this tendency.

ENGINE
Petronas SPE 04A
Number of cylinders : 10 V 80degree
Capacity : 2997 cc
Power : 800 bhp
Weight : 110 kg

RED BULL SAUBER PETRONA

Tyres Bridgestone
Address : Red Bull Sauber AG
Wildbachstrasse 9
8340 Hinwil
Switzerland
Tel : + 41 (0) 1 938 83 00
Fax : + 41 (0) 1 938 83 01
Web-site : www.redbull-sauber.ch
Team principal : Peter Sauber
Technical director : Leo Ress
Employees : 210
G.P. debut : South Africa 1993
G.P. participations : 113
0 wins, 0 pole positions
Number of points scored : 84 points
Best position in World Constructors' championship: 6th in 1998
Best position in World Drivers' championship: 9th in 1995 (Frentzen)
Test driver : Enrique Bernoldi (Brazil)
1999 position: 8th (5 points)

Peter Sauber

Leo Ress

- Strengthened technical team 5000 km of winter testing	- Rivalry between drivers
- Good engine-gearbox compromise	- Old generation engine
- Adequate budget	- Team isolated in Switzerland
	- No major manufacturer as partner

G.P. debut: Brazil 1995 (Forti)
Best position in World Driver's championship: 14th in 1998 (Arrows)
82 Grand Prix participations, 10 points scored, 0 wins, 0 pole position
F1 record:
-1995 : Forti, 0 point
-1996 : Ligier, 2 points, 15th in championship
-1997 : Arrows, 2 points, 16th in championship
-1998 : Arrows, 3 points, 14th in championship
-1999 : Sauber, 3 points, 14th in championship

PEDRO DINIZ

RED BULL SAUBER PETRONAS

Pedro Diniz is about to tackle his sixth season in Formula One. Tanned, handsome, with the look of a playboy, he's found it difficult to shake off the tag of 'paying driver.' He's had the good fortune to have benefited from the unconditional support of Parmalat since his arrival in the top division of motor sport.

Peter Sauber may not be a philanthropist, and probably finds the millions of dollars brought by the Italian producer of dairy products useful, but even so, he has chosen to retain the services of his Brazilian driver for his talent behind the wheel.

Last year, in spite of a car which was frequently let down by its gearbox, he managed to score three World Championship points in good races.

The progression of Pedro Diniz is constant. If the Sauber C 19 matches his own talents, then one could certainly see the Brazilian scoring points, and why not on the occasional rostrum?

He gets on well with the team, with whom he has been now for a couple of years. Mika Salo's presence will almost certainly provide extra motivation for a driver who could quite easily have opted for a gentleman driver's role, but instead swapped restaurants and night clubs for technical briefings and physical training.

First car driven?
A VW Beetle when I was nine.

Your personal car?
A Mercedes SL73.

Favourite or dream car?
Ferrari 550.

Most memorable race car?
The 1996 Ligier-Honda with which I scored my first points, and this year's Sauber C19.

Sweetest racing memory?
I think it's still Spa in 1997 when I was third in the race at one time.

Worst racing memory?
My spectacular accident at Nurburgring last year.

Your favourite circuit?
Barcelona.

Your least favourite circuit?
None in particular.

Which driver from the past do you admire most?
Ayrton Senna.

Which current driver do you admire most?
Michael Schumacher.

Your favourite food?
Pasta and more precisely spaghetti a la 'crudaiola'.

Favourite drink?
Mineral water.

What sport do you do?
Cycling, jogging, squash, cross-country skiing and all water sports.

What are your favourite sports?
Tennis.

Who is your favourite sportsman?
The American golfer Tiger Woods who is winning all the big tournaments.

What are your hobbies?
Going out in my boat. And like all Brazilians, I love the sun!

Your favourite films?
I loved 'It's a wonderful Life' with Roberto Benigni.

Favourite actors?
I like Bruce Willis.

What do you watch on television?
Television bores me.

What's your favourite colour?
Blue.

Favourite music?
Sade, 'soft' rock with perhaps a slight preference for the music of Brazilian groups.

What do you read?
Good thrillers.

What is your goal in racing?
To have fun

Outside motor racing, whom do you admire?
Top sportsman.

If you had to be marooned on a desert island, who or what would you take with you?
My girlfriend Cassia.

What do you think is the most important thing in life?
To be happy.

What is it that fascinates you about your profession?
Driving race cars.

What don't you like about it?
The pressure.

What are your best qualities?
In racing, it's the speed.

What are your faults?
I'm Latin, so sometimes I'm a bit impulsive!

Have you thought what you are going to do after Formula One?
I think I'll stay in racing.

Date of birth : May 22 1970
Place : Sao Paulo (Brazil)
Nationality : Brazilian
Residence : Sao Paulo and Monte Carlo
Marital status : girlfriend Cassia
Height : 1.74 m
Weight : 69 kg
Web-site : www.pedrodiniz.com

Grand Prix debut: Japan 1994 (Lotus)
Best position in World Drivers' Championship : 10th in 1999
(BAR and Ferrari)
78 Grand Prix participations, 25 points scored, 0 wins, 0 pole position
F1 record:
-1994 : Lotus, (2 G.Ps. entered), 0 point
-1995 : Tyrrell, 5 points, 14th in championship
-1996 : Tyrrell, 5 points, 13th in championship
-1997 : Tyrrell, 2 points, 16th in championship
-1998 : Arrows, 3 points, 13th in championship
-1999 : BAR and Ferrari (9 G.Ps. entered), 10 points, 10th in championship

MIKA SALO

RED BULL SAUBER PETRONAS

A few weeks before the start of last season, Mika Salo found himself without a drive. He learned that the Arrows team had decided to sign Toranosuke Takagi and his suitcases of yen rather than the Finn. But one man's bad luck can soon become another man's good luck. Having stepped in to replace the injured Ricardo Zonta at BAR, he was asked to do the same for the injured Michael Schumacher at Ferrari.

At Hockenheim, he led the race from Eddie Irvine. He could have won easily, but instead let the Irishman do so, for Eddie was disputing the World Championship. The Scuderia deeply appreciated this gesture. Less than an month later, it was learned that Mika Salo would be driving for Sauber in 2000, the Swiss team acting as a kind of satellite for Ferrari. In one race, the Finn had sealed his future and kick-started his career.

Like Sauber, he needed to rebuild his reputation. The Swiss car of the new era should allow him to do that.

First car driven?
I must have been six years old. It was on my father's knee, in my grandfather's garden and the car was a Datsun 100 A.

Your personal car?
A Ferrari F50, an Audi S3 and a Plymouth 'Hot Rod'.

Favourite or dream car?
None in particular.

Most memorable race car?
Last year's Ferrari F399.

Sweetest racing memory?
My relaxed and carefree days in Formula Ford.

Worst racing memory?
Certainly Spa in 1998. I crashed two cars in practice and wasn't able to start the race.

Your favourite circuit?
Suzuka.

Your least favourite circuit?
Fuji.

Which driver from the past do you admire most?
James Hunt.

Which current driver do you admire most?
David Coulthard and Jacques Villeneuve are good friends.

Your favourite food?
Pasta.

Favourite drink?
Milk.

What sport do you do?
Physical training, cycling, snowboarding and snowmobiles in Finland.

What are your favourite sports?
Ice hockey and snowboarding competitions.

Who is your favourite sportsman?
I like the ice hockey players, and one in particular, Teemu Selanne.

What are your hobbies?
I love music and mainly hard rock. I've got thousands of CDs and I like playing the guitar.

Your favourite films?
Action films and all the James Bond films.

Favourite actors?
Meg Ryan and all actresses...

What do you watch on television?
I like flitting from programme to programme.

What's your favourite colour?
Blue.

Favourite music?
Led Zeppelin, AC/DC and hard rock in general.

What do you read?
Comic strips.

What is your goal in racing?
To satisfy my desire to drive.

Outside motor racing, whom do you admire?
Too many people to mention here.

If you had to be marooned on a desert island, who or what would you take with you?
Lots of things to eat and my wife Noriko.

What do you think is the most important thing in life?
Health.

What is it that fascinates you about your profession?
The freedom.

What don't you like about it?
The travelling and the politics.

What are your best qualities?
That's for you to tell me!

What are your faults?
Lots of nasty things.

Have you thought what you are going to do after Formula One?
I don't know yet.

Date of birth: November 30 1966
Place: Helsinki (Finland)
Nationality : Finnish
Residence : London (England)
Marital status : married to Noriko
Height : 1.75 m
Weight : 66 kg
Web-site : www.mikasalo.net

ARROWS F1 TEAM

ENGINE
Supertec FB02
Number of cylinders : 10 V 71degree
Capacity : 2998 cc
Power : 780 bhp
Weight : 117 kg

ARROWS F1 TEAM

Arrows A21
Tyres Bridgestone
Address : Arrows F1 Team
Leafield Technical , NR Witney
Oxon OX8 5PF
England
Tel : (00 44) 19 93 87 10 00
Fax : (00 44) 19 93 87 11 00
Internet : www.arrows.com
Team principal : Tom Walkinshaw
Technical director : Mike Coughlan
Employees : 200
G.P. debut: Australia : Brésil 1978
G.P. participations : 337
Number of victories : 0
Number of pole positions : 1
Number of points scored : 157 points
Best position in World Constructors' championship :
4 ème en 1988
Best position in World Drivers' championship :
7 ème en 1988 (D. Warwick)
1999 position : 9 ème (1 points)
Test driver : Mark Webber (Australie)

The Arrows team has suffered from a lack of competitivity for a number of years now. After attracting attention thanks to the presence and sometimes the performances of Damon Hill, the team from Leafield had rather sunk into obscurity again last year.
This year, however, they've bounced back, having swapped the rather underpowered Arrows nee Hart engine for a more powerful and more expensive Supertec engine. Right from the first test, Pedro de la Rosa and the returning Jos Verstappen have proved that the new A21 is very competitive.
And Tom Walkinshaw revealed that he'd capitalised on it when the team was finally launched officially in Melbourne. Several new sponsors from the world of telecommunications and the Internet had joined Arrows. The figures were impressive.
So Uncle Tom is expecting qualifying results inside the top ten followed by race results earning points. They had suspension problems at Melbourne which scuppered the plan, but those should be quickly cured.

Tom Walkinshaw

Mike Coughlan

+	−
- Supertec engine better than Arrows unit - Good technical team - Increased budget - Good car - Good drivers - Motivation	- No support from major manufacturer - No history

G.P. debut: Australia 1999 (Arrows)
16 Grand Prix participations, 1 point scored, 0 wins,
0 pole position
-1992 British Formula Renault champion
-1995 Japanese F3 champion
-1997 Japanese GT champion (Toyota)
-1997 Japanese F3000 champion

PEDRO DE LA ROSA

Arrows F1 Team

Pedro de la Rosa is embarking on his second Formula One season, once again with Arrows. Last year, this 29-year old scored the first point of his career in his first Grand Prix, just as Alain Prost had done in Argentina in 1980. But it was the team's only point of the year. Driving a car that was scarcely competitive, and not very reliable, it was difficult to show his true value. This year, with a better engine, the Supertec, and a more competitive chassis, he should be able to move up the Formula One hierarchy. He's still supported by the Spanish petrol company Repsol who helped him into Formula One at the same time as his Catalan compatriot Marc Gene.

His patron Tom Walkinshaw says of him, "he's an intelligent guy and he knows that the situation has now changed at Arrows, and that he has to be competitive in all circumstances."

After spending the first season learning and gaining precious experience, the Spanish driver now has to confirm the hopes placed in him.

First car driven?
A Renault 5 when I was nine.

Your personal car?
Honda Prelude

Favourite or dream car?
Les Porsche 911

Most memorable race car?
The 1997 Formula Nippon Lola.

Sweetest racing memory?
My first victorie in Formule Nippon in Suzuka in 1997

Worst racing memory?
My saison in F3 1994 in Great Britain

Your favourite circuit?
Suzuka.

Your least favourite circuit?
Tsukuba in Japan, which is a kart circuit they use for F3.

Which driver from the past do you admire most?
Ayrton Senna.

Which current driver do you admire most?
Michael Schumacher.

Your favourite food?
Pasta and paella. I hate English food.

Favourite drink?
Mineral water.

What sport do you do?
Cycling, jogging, weight training, squash, karting and sailing.

What are your favourite sports?
Football and FC Barcelona in particular.

Who is your favourite sports man?
The rally driver Carlos Sainz who is a hero in Spain.

What are your hobbies?
Every sport

Your favourite films?
Films that don't make you think too much. For me, a film should be relaxing.

Favourite actors?
Anthony Hopkins and Meg Ryan.

What do you watch on television?
Certain films and sport.

What's your favourite colour?
Red and blue.

Favourite music?
The Spanish group Mecano.

What do you read?
Adventure books and biographies.

What is your goal in racing?
To be World Champion.

Outside motor racing, whom do you admire?
My girlfriend Maria, my friends and my family.

If you had to be marooned on a desert island, who or what would you take with you?
Maria, my family and some food.

What do you think is the most important thing in life?
To be happy and to have an objective.

What is it that fascinates you about your profession?
I like it all.

What don't you like about it?
The travelling is tiring.

What are your best qualities?
I am opinionated.

What are your faults?
I understand other people too well and I don't listen to them.

Have you thought what you are going to do after Formula One?
I'm going to help out in the family business.

Date of birth : February 24 1971
Place : Barcelona (Spain)
Nationality : Spanish
Residence : Barcelona
Marital status : girlfriend Maria
Height : 1.77 m
Weight : 75 kg
Web-site : www.pedrodelarosa.com

aGrand Prix debut: Brazil 1994 (Benetton)
Best position in World Drivers' Championship : 10th in 1994 (Benetton)
57 Grand Prix participations, 11 points scored, 0 wins, 0 pole position
-1993 German F3 champion
-1993 Winner of F3 Marlboro Masters at Zandvoort
F1 record:
-1994 : Benetton, (10 G.Ps. entered), 10 points, 10th in championship
-1995 : Simtek, (5 G.Ps. entered), 0 point
-1996 : Arrows, 1 point, 16th in championship
-1997 : Tyrrell, 0 point
-1998 : Stewart, (9 G.Ps. entered), 0 point

JOS VERSTAPPEN

Arrows F1 Team

Jos Verstappen was to some extent considered a great new hope after winning the German F3 Championship and the Marlboro Masters at Zandvoort in 1993.

He was suddenly called up to team up alongside Michael Schumacher at Benetton, and thrust into the limelight when his Benetton caught fire spectacularly during refuelling at Hockenheim - suddenly everyone knew of Jos Verstappen. And in spite of his inexperience, he twice finished third, in Hungary and Belgium.

Unfortunately, what came next was less glorious. 'Jos the Boss' as his Dutch fans nicknamed him, could never come to terms with the less competitive machinery in which he found himself. He couldn't even relaunch his career in the rapid Stewart in 1998 although he certainly showed promise and speed last year as test driver for the Honda F1 project.

This is almost certainly his last chance in Formula One. As team boss Tom Walkinshaw puts it, "Jos is conscious of the problems and the situation. If he doesn't make it this season, he'd better go looking for a drive in the national touring car championship."

After a career of ups and downs, Verstappen now has to face up to his responsibilities.

First car driven?
I must have been 10 years old, but I can't remember what kind of car it was.

Your personal car?
Mercedes CLK

Favourite or dream car?
It was a Porsche 993 which I sold.

Most memorable race car?
This year's Arrows A21.

Sweetest racing memory?
I haven't had many. They are still to come.

Worst racing memory?
Hockenheim in 1994. I had to qualify in Michael Schumacher's car, and on Sunday, my Benetton burst into flames during refuelling.

Your favourite circuit?
Spa.

Your least favourite circuit?
None.

Which driver from the past do you admire most?
Niki Lauda and Senna who I would have liked to have known better.

Which current driver do you admire most?
Michael Schumacher.

Your favourite food?
Pasta and Dutch cooking.

Favourite drink?
Coca Cola.

What sport do you do?
Physical training, squash and road cycling.

What are your favourite sports?
Karting.

Who is your favourite sportsman?
I'm impressed by Janni Romme, a Dutch speed skater.

What are your hobbies?
I have a business making kart engines. And I have a team or young drivers aged from 12 to 18, one of whom finished second in the World Championship.

Your favourite films?
Action films, and principally 'The Negotiator'.

Favourite actors?
None in particular.

What do you watch on television?
I'm never at home to watch it! I only see it in hotels.

What's your favourite colour?
Dark blue.

Favourite music?
Principally pop music.

What do you read?
I don't have time to read.

What is your goal in racing?
To win Grands Prix.

Outside motor racing, whom do you admire?
I like politics.

If you had to be marooned on a desert island, who or what would you take with you?
Some water...

What do you think is the most important thing in life?
To be in good health, and to do your job well.

What is it that fascinates you about your profession?
The magic of Formula 1.

What don't you like about it?
The politics and the importance of money.

What are your best qualities?
I'm sensitive, relaxed and I never get upset.

What are your faults?
Too many!

Have you thought what you are going to do after Formula One?
Stay in motor racing and have some fun.

Date of birth : March 4 1972
Place : Montford (Holland)
Nationality : Dutch
Residence : Montford (Holland) and Monte Carlo.
Marital status : married to Sophie
Height : 1.75 m
Weight : 73 kg
Web-site : www.verstappen.com

TELEFONICA MINARDI
FONDMETAL

ENGINE :
FONDMETAL V10 (base Ford
Cosworth)
Number of cylinders : 10 V 72 degree
Capacity : 2998 cc
Power : 740 bhp
Weight : 124 kilos

Because it doesn't have the support of a major manufacturer, the little Minardi team has to buy in its engine deal. For a long time, they hoped that they might get a Supertec thanks to the support of their new best friends at Telefonica, the Spanish telecommunications giant, but instead, they had to fall back on an ex-Stewart Ford engine which team boss Gabriele Rumi christened after his Fondmetal business. But the construction of the Minardi M02 had already been badly delayed.

It ran for the first time at Barcelona on February 17, and immediately proved to be competitive in spite of the 100 horsepower deficit in comparison to its rivals. At Melbourne, there was a surprise, for while everyone knew that Marc Gené was a good driver, they also discovered that his teammate Gaston Mazzacane wasn't devoid of talent either. Even so, it will be tough for the little team to score points, under any circumstances. However, the Minardi team has already won one trophy, that for achievement.

For with a budget ten times less than its compatriot Ferrari, the Minardi team always attracts deepest respect from a huge following worldwide.

TELEFONICA MINARDI FONDMETAL

TELEFONICA MINARDI FONDMETAL Minardi M02
Address : Minardi Team Spa
Via Spallanzani 21, Z.I.
48018 Faenza (Ra)
Italy
Tel : + 39 0546 69 61 11
Fax : + 39 0546 62 09 98
Web-site : www.minardi.it
Team principal: Gabriele Rumi
Technical director : Gustav Brunner
Employees : 140
G.P. debut: Brazil 1985
G.P. participations : 237
0 wins, 0 pole position
Number of points scored : 28
Best position in World Constructors' championship :
7th in 1991
Best position in World Drivers' championship :
Martini (7th in 1991)
Test driver : Fernando Alonso (Spain)
1999 position: 1 point (10th)

Gabriele Rumi

Gustav Brunner

+		-
- Increased budget	- Limited means	
- Good technical team	- Old style engine	
- Enthusiasm and motivation	- No partnership with a major manufacturer	
- Good drivers	- Car ready too late	

G.P. debut: Australia 1999 (Minardi)
16 Grand Prix participations, 1 point, 0 wins, 0 pole position
-1998 Formula Open Nissan Fortuna champion
F1 record:
-1999 : Minardi, 1 point, 18th in championship

MARC GENÉ

TELEFONICA MINARDI FONDMETAL

Marc Gene had just won the first Formula Open Nissan championship when, in December 1998, at Barcelona, a few kilometres from his home, he tested for Minardi, with a number of other young drivers.

Perhaps thanks to his degree in economics from universities in Spain and England, he managed to persuade the telecommunications giant Telefonica to support him at Minardi.

Many thought that the Spanish driver would be out of his depth. Driving for the smallest team in the championship, they thought he would be outclassed by his teammate, Luca Badoer, who was and is the current test driver for Ferrari. But Marc Gene was one of the surprises of the year. Not only did he match Badoer but frequently qualified ahead of him. He even scored a point, which was quite a feat in an underpowered car such as his, and qualified an excellent fifteenth at Hockenheim. The friendly little Minardi team has renewed its confidence in Marc again in 2000 when he has the opportunity to continue his progression.

First car driven?
A red, 1.3 litre Ford Fiesta when I was 13.

Your personal car?
A Peugeot 406 Coupe and a Porsche Carrera 4 loaned to me by a friend.

Favourite or dream car?
Porsche bi-turbo.

Most memorable race car?
The 1999 Minardi M 01 at the end of last year.

Sweetest racing memory?
The first day that I drove a Formula One car, the first lap, the feelings...

Worst racing memory?
An accident at Pau in 1997 in F3000 when my sponsors abandoned me, and my retirement on the grid at Barcelona in 1999.

Your favourite circuit?
Barcelona.

Your least favourite circuit?
Jarama.

Which driver from the past do you admire most?
My brother Jordi was always an inspiration to me.

Which current driver do you admire most?
The current generation of Villeneuve, Coulthard, Fisichella and Barrichello.

Your favourite food?
Pasta and paella Valenciana.

Favourite drink?
Mineral water and milk.

What sport do you do?
Physical preparation, climbing, karting, diving, tennis and mountain biking.

What are your favourite sports?
Motor sports, tennis and basketball.

Who is your favourite sportsman?
Spanish tennis players like Alex Corretja.

What are your hobbies?
Reading novels, cinema and playing sport.

Your favourite films?
I saw a film with Val Kilmer recently which I liked, but generally speaking, action films.

Favourite actors?
Al Pacino, Robert de Niro, Uma Thurman and Jodie Foster.

What do you watch on television?
News programmes.

What's your favourite colour?
Silver grey.

Favourite music?
Dire Straits, The Cardigans and I like everything from classic rock to techno and black music.

What do you read?
Newspapers, news and sports magazines as well as historical books and biographies.

What is your goal in racing?
After scoring my first point in 1999, I'm looking to do better.

Outside motor racing, whom do you admire?
Certain politicians.

If you had to be marooned on a desert island, who or what would you take with you?
If there was already something to eat, I would take a box of books.

What do you think is the most important thing in life?
To be happy with oneself.

What is it that fascinates you about your profession?
Seeking perfection, which isn't easy.

What don't you like about it?
The importance of money.

What are your best qualities?
My head.

What are your faults?
I'm too much of a perfectionist.

Have you thought what you are going to do after Formula One?
It will certainly be in business.

Date of birth : March 29 1974
Place : Sabadell (Spain)
Nationality : Spanish
Residence : Bellaterra (suburb of Barcelona)
Marital status : bachelor
Height : 1.73 m
Weight : 69 kg
Web-site :
www.marcgene.com

G.P. debut: Australia 2000 (Minardi)
-1994 Italian F2000 champion

GASTON MAZZACANE

TELEFONICA MINARDI FONDMETAL

Esteban Tuero was the last Argentine in Formula One. He came from nowhere and returned there just as quickly, in 1998. Now Gaston Mazzacane has appeared, to pick up the second drive at Minardi this year.

Telefonica, the telecommunication multi-national and partner to the team, wanted an Argentine driver to help open new markets in the country. The 25-year old youngster beat compatriot and former Formula One driver Norberto Fontana to the drive, to make his Formula One debut.

Mazzacane was the Minardi test driver last year, so he wasn't exactly a newcomer to the team or car. But he was willing and determined. But how would he react to the jungle that is F1? After all, his record isn't staggering. In two seasons of F3000, he has scored a single point in a race that was decimated by retirements.

His one moment of glory was a win at Magny-Cours in a sports car race last year, driving a Ferrari 333 SP shared with former Minardi driver Giovanni Lavaggi.

They say that he is impulsive, frequently involved in accidents. But over the years, Giancarlo Fisichella and Jarno Trulli have both used their debut drives with Minardi to lead to better things with stronger teams. Could Gaston Mazzacane use this opportunity as a similar stepping stone?

First car driven?
A Ford Taunus when I was ten.

Your personal car?
BMW M3.

Favourite or dream car?
Ferrari 360 Modena.

Most memorable race car?
The Ferrari 333 SP in which I won at Magny-Cours in 1999 and of course, the Minardi.

Sweetest racing memory?
Magny-Cours in the rain last year, and a win at Monza in 2000 in 1994.

Worst racing memory?
F3000 Hockenheim in the rain in 1998 when I was involved in a nine car pile-up.

Your favourite circuit?
Interlagos, Mugello and Spa.

Your least favourite circuit?
Brno in Czechoslovakia.

Which driver from the past do you admire most?
Fangio, Reutemann, Senna and Schumacher at their peak.

Which current driver do you admire most?
Obviously Michael Schumacher and I know Fisichella, Trulli and Gene well.

Your favourite food?
L'asado, an Argentine meat speciality, and pasta.

Favourite drink?
Squeezed orange juice, mineral water and beer.

What sport do you do?
Karting, mountain bike, water-skiing and body-board.

What are your favourite sports?
Football and particularly the Argentine club River Plate.

Who is your favourite sportsman?
Diego Maradona when he was playing, and Gabriel Batistuta of Fiorentina.

What are your hobbies?
Exploring, visiting places that I don't know, shopping, strolling. I'm also going to support the Minardi football team whose ground is across the road from where I live in Faenza.

Favourite films?
A film has to be a diversion for me. I liked 'Jerry McGuire' with Tom Cruise.

Favourite actors?
I prefer actresses like Demi Moore.

What do you watch on television?
Mainly films.

What's your favourite colour?
Red.

Favourite music?
Rock, the Rolling Stones, U2, Red Hot Chili Peppers, and Argentine groups like los Bedondos and Ratones Paranoicos.

What do you read?
Motoring magazines.

What is your goal in racing?
I always wanted to get into F1. Now I want to stay here.

Outside motor racing, whom do you admire?
I like to talk with my father.

If you had to be marooned on a desert island, who or what would you take with you?
Extra water and a girlfriend.

What do you think is the most important thing in life?
To get to where you dream of going.

What fascinates you about your profession?
Being on the limit and constantly learning to be more professional.

What don't you like about it?
Travelling.

What are your best qualities?
Knowing to wait and choosing the right moment.

What are your faults?
I'm too demanding.

Have you thought what you are going to do after Formula One?
Stay in motor sport and assist the promotion of young Argentine drivers into Formula One.

Date of birth : May 8 1975
Place : La Plata (Argentina)
Nationality : Argentine
Residence : La Plata
(Argentina) and Faenza (Italy)
Marital status : bachelor
Height : 1.73 m
Weight : 69 kg

BRITISH AMERICAN RACING

ENGINE

Honda RA 000 E V10
Number of cylinders : 10 V 72 degree
Capacity : 2999 cc
Power : 810 bhp
Weight : 105 kilos

BAR were their own worst enemy; the expectations of their first year were too great. Last year, with optimism ringing in their ears, unreliability made British American Racing's debut year catastrophic.

The team suffered hugely from its youth and its own hype, unable to score a single point, and finishing last in the World Championship, in spite of a huge budget, riven with internal quarrels and individual ambitions.

In spite of this disappointment, team principal Craig Pollock succeeded in getting Honda to join them for better or for worse in 2000.

The BAR 002 was ready before Christmas, and while it wasn't particularly quick, it was reliable, and that's exactly what both parties wanted.

And in Melbourne, driver Jacques Villeneuve reappeared at the front of the field from the start of practice, as though boosted by the Japanese engine behind him. In the race, the Canadian driver confirmed his performance with an excellent fourth place, while teammate Ricardo Zonta came home sixth. For some, this result was one of the surprises of the start of the season, but the performance had always been there, and so, now too, the reliability.

The 1997 World Champion hadn't lost his sense of humour during the bad times. "Now at least, we're almost certainly not to finish last in the championship," he said after Melbourne.

BRITISH AMERICAN RACING

■ BRITISH AMERICAN RACING HONDA BAR PR 02
Tyres Bridgestone
Address : British American Racing
Brackley, Northamptonshire, NN13 7BD
England
Tel : + 44 (0) 12 80 84 40 00
Fax : + 44 (0) 12 80 84 40 01
Web-site : www.britishamericanracing.com
Team principal : Craig Pollock
Technical director : Dr. Adrian Reynard
Employees : 280
G.P. debut: Australia 1999
G.P. participations : 16
0 wins, 0 pole position, 0 points
Test driver : Darren Manning (England)
Development driver : Patrick Lemarie (France)

Craig Pollock

Malcom Oastler

+	−
- Very good budget	- Relations between Pollock and Reynard
- Honda comes on board	- A disastrous 1999 season
- Jacques Villeneuve	- Lack of experience
- Car ready in December 1999	
- Motivation	

G.P. debut: Australia 1996 (Williams)
World Drivers' champion in 1997 (Williams)
64 Grand Prix participations, 180 points scored,
11 wins, 13 pole positions
-1995 IndyCar Champion in USA
-1995 Winner of Indianapolis 500
F1 record:
-1996 : Williams, 78 points, 2nd in championship
-1997 : Williams, 81 points, World Champion
-1998 : Williams, 21 points, 5th in championship
-1999 : BAR, 0 point

JACQUES VILLENEUVE

BRITISH AMERICAN RACING

World Champion in 1997, it seems that Jacques Villeneuve didn't want to miss out on the crazy adventure that his friend Craig Pollock was embarking on. Creating a new team with great ambition was an exciting and fascinating challenge.

So he went into it with eyes wide open, and took the brickbats, the disappointments, suffered the retirements and midfield grid positions. He only saw the chequered flag once, and that was in the last Grand Prix of the season in Japan.

But it made no difference to the way he drove races. He didn't let up once. He was still always on the limit, sometimes over it to compensate for the car's weaknesses. His professionalism was without reproach. He never gave up, always did his best. And eventually he could see the light at the end of the tunnel. The arrival of Honda and the experience acquired by the team should allow Jacques Villeneuve to begin to drink success after a year of abstinence.

He's a pleasant guy. Son of Gilles Villeneuve, he has cultivated a sense of difference. His clothes are different, he changes the colour of his hair. It livens up the paddock. Like his friend David Coulthard, he is in the only other driver to sleep in his own motorhome at the circuit during a Grand Prix. Thankfully, not all Grand Prix drivers come out of the same mould.

The year 2000 may not see Jacques Villeneuve permanently back in the winner's circle, but it will see him back in the points. And it will be the end of the drought for the guy who shows not only panache on the track, but in the paddock too.

First car driven?
A Fiat Uno when I was 18. I hit a gendarme after going through a stop sign!

Your personal car?
Audi A8, Chevrolet Camaro and Chevrolet Pick-Up 1957

Favourite or dream car?
A Dodge Viper.

Most memorable race car?
The 1997 Williams with which I won the World Championship.

Sweetest racing memory?
Jerez in 1997 and my win at Indianapolis in 1995.

Worst racing memory?
Phoenix in F. Atlantic in 1994 when I cut my car in two!

Your favourite circuit?
Elkart Lake in the USA.

Your least favourite circuit?
Detroit.

Which driver from the past do you admire most?
I don't have any heroes, but I had a lot of admiration for Ayrton Senna.

Which current drivers do you like most?
Mika Salo and David Coulthard are good friends.

Your favourite food?
Pasta.

Favourite drink?
Milk and root beer.

What sport do you do?
Alpine skiing, roller blading and physical training.

What are your favourite sports?
Alpine skiing and ice hockey.

Who is your favourite sportsman?
Downhill skiers are fantastic, particularly at Kitzbuhel. Generally speaking, I like people who take part in risky sports.

What are your hobbies?
I love skiing, the guitar, computers and reading.

Your favourite films?
I love "Le Diner de Cons".

Favourite actors?
Val Kilmer, Christian Slater and Meg Ryan.

What do you watch on television?
The pop station MTV for their music clips.

What's your favourite colour?
Blue, brown, green and black.

Favourite music?
Senisonic, Rushmore et Taxiride un groupe australien

What do you read?
Science fiction books.

What is your goal in racing?
It's very simple: to win.

Outside motor racing, whom do you admire?
No one in particular.

If you had to be marooned on a desert island, who or what would you take with you?
My girlfriend Dannii

What do you think is the most important thing in life?
The protection of one's private life. I like to be myself.

What is it that fascinates you about your profession?
The danger, being on the edge, driving at the limit.

What don't you like about it?
I hate doing promotions.

What are your best qualities?
Sincerity and spontaneity. I like to be myself.

What are your faults?
I am very egotistical and untidy.

Have you thought what you are going to do after Formula One?
Play and compose music.

Date of birth : April 9 1971
Place : St Jean sur Richelieu (Canada)
Nationality : Canadian
Residence : Monte Carlo
Marital status : girlfriend Dannii
Height : 1.71 m
Weight : 63 kg
Web-site : www.jacques-ville-neuve.com

G.P. debut : Australia 1999 (BAR)
-1997 International F3000 champion
-1998 World GT champion (Mercedes)
12 Grand Prix participations, 0 points, 0 wins, 0 pole position
F1 record:
-1999 : BAR, 0 point

RICARDO ZONTA

BRITISH AMERICAN RACING

Ricardo Zonta is used to being on the rostrum. After winning the F3000 title in 1997, he joined the Mercedes team, and became World GT champion driving a huge Mercedes CLK which positively oozed horsepower.

That same year, 1998, he began to drive in Formula One as test driver for McLaren. Still under contract with McLaren-Mercedes, he made his F1 with the new BAR team beside Jacques Villeneuve. But in Brazil, he injured his foot in a big accident, and missed four races. On his return, performance and reliability were still lacking in the young team, and Craig Pollock's team structure did tend to focus on Villeneuve's car.

Under these circumstances, learning wasn't easy. He rarely benefited from the latest developments which usually seemed to go to his teammate. Nevertheless, he was never far behind in terms of pure performance. In spite of this difficult year, in year 2000, Ricardo Zonta continues his apprenticeship with British American Racing. This smiling young 24-year old Brazilian, affable but almost shy, still hasn't reached his true potential. If the BAR-Honda is competitive, then you can be sure that the young man from Curitiba will get there.

First car driven?
A Ford Galaxy on the knee of my father when I was three.

Your personal car?
Honda S2000

Favourite or dream car?
The Mercedes CLK which I have in Brazil.

Most memorable race car?
I hope that that will be the 2000 BAR-Honda!

Sweetest racing memory?
Becoming a Formula One driver.

Worst racing memory?
Retiring from leading in F3000 at Jerez.

Your favourite circuit?
Mugello.

Your least favourite circuit?
The Helsinki circuit that we used in ITC and Dijon which is so dangerous because of the bumps.

Which driver from the past do you admire most?
Ayrton Senna.

Which current driver to like most?
Barrichello and Diniz are good friends.

Your favourite food?
Pasta with chicken.

Favourite drink?
Real orange juice from Brazil.

What sport do you do?
Physical training, water skiing and all water sports.

What are your favourite sports?
Water sports.

Who's your favourite sportsman?
No one in particular.

What are your hobbies?
Water Skiing, surf and video games.

Your favourite films?
Adventure films like 'Braveheart'.

Favourite actors?
Meg Ryan in "La cite des anges".

What do you watch on television?
I only really watch it at home in Brazil.

What's your favourite colour?
Anthracite grey.

Favourite music?
The Corrs and the Brazilian group Paralamas do sucesso.

What do you read?
I don't like reading.

What is your goal in racing?
To become World Champion.

Outside motor racing, whom do you admire?
My father and my family.

If you had to be marooned on a desert island, who or what would you take with you?
A pretty girl!

What do you think is the most important thing in life?
To believe in God.

What is it that fascinates you about your profession?
Racing and driving.

What don't you like about it?
Endless travelling.

What are your best qualities?
I'm calm and determined.

What are your faults?
I'm too shy.

Have you thought what you are going to do after Formula One?
Work in my father's business.

Date of birth : March 23 1976
Place : Curitiba (Brazil)
Nationality : Brazilian
Residence : Monte Carlo
Marital status : bachelor
Height : 1.72 m
Weight : 65 kg
Web-site:
www.ricardozonta.com.br

Magazine

ON THE TECHNICAL FRONT

2001 will be the year of important technical reforms. However, this year, the rules are very stable. Nevertheless, there are some details which have been modified.

Apart from the cockpit, the width of the lateral protection has been increased.

not done in a dangerous manner, before the pole position car has taken up its position on the starting grid.

In the case of rain, the race director can stop a car if its rear light is not working. It will only be allowed to re-start when the fault is cured.

There will now be two driver briefings on the first day of practice: one at 10h00 and one at 17h00.

If a car breaks down during free practice and is brought back to the pits by the marshals, during a free practice session, it can no longer be used during that session. If this rule is broken, the best qualifying time will be cancelled.

In the case of a breakdown during qualifying, if the driver gets back to the pits before his car, he will have to be weighed. Only then will he be allowed out in the spare car. This is so that it can be established that the total weight is not less than 600 kilos when the car is brought back. Anyone not complying with this rule will have their best qualifying time cancelled

Eddie Irvine wanted to lead a team. Now he is Number 1 at Jaguar on double his previous salary. It's the deal of the year.

Jean Alesi's dream comes true. He will drive for his old mate Alain Prost.

Jarno Trulli does a good deal and finds himself at the wheel of a very competitive Jordan.

The arrivals:

International F3000 champion, Nick Heidfeld is Jean Alesi's team mate at Prost.

Jenson Button is only 20 and on a phenomenal rise to the top. He only started racing ten years ago and now he drives for Williams.

Gaston Mazzacane comes to Minardi. Nothing is known about him. Will he be up to it?

Jos Verstappen breaks a long lean spell with a return to F1 at Arrows. Could it be his last chance?

WHAT HAS CHANGED IN 2000

The safety roll-over hoop behind the driver's head has been strengthened. This change came about after Pedro Diniz's accident at the Nurburgring last year. His car rolled over in spectacular fashion and the hoop was ripped off.

The crash test for the survival cell has been made tougher, in order to further improve driver safety.

There will be more checks on the dimensions of the flat bottom and the skid plates.

On the fuel front, there will be a reduction in the percentage of sulphur permitted, in line with new standards for Eurosuper.

The on-board electronics has to be validated by FIA before the start of the season. Checks will be carried out to detect any driver aids which are strictly banned (traction control, anti-lock brakes and anti-spin.)

ON THE SPORTING FRONT

The speed limit in the pit lane is now down to 60 km/h during practice and 80 km/h during the race and warm-up. In Monaco, the limit will be 60 km/h all weekend.

From now on, a car delayed on the formation lap will be able to regain its position as long as it is

ON THE HUMAN FRONT

The transfers:

Rubens Barrichello has left Stewart to become Michael Schumacher's team mate at Ferrari. A major challenge.

After a great job as a locum at Ferrari, Mika Salo found a berth with Sauber.

The departures:

Damon Hill definitely retired one year too late. He ran out of motivation last year and was dominated by team mate Frentzen.

Alessandro Zanardi was another victim of Williams politics. He was shown the door without much of an explanation.

Toranosuke Takagi chose to return home to Japan to contest the Formula Nippon series.

Olivier Panis was in crisis. Now he has a great chance to rebuild his career as McLaren's third driver.

Luca Badoer quit driving for Minardi to concentrate on his job as Ferrari's test driver.

Jackie Stewart decided to step back from the controls, having sold his team to Ford, who turned it into Jaguar. He wants to spend more time with his family.

ON A MORE GENERAL NOTE

After a glorious past in F1, first in the Sixties and then with Williams and McLaren, Honda is back in business as BAR's new partner.

BMW used to be in F1 from 1982 to 1987 and it has now returned to partner Williams with a big budget.

Jaguar has a great track record in long distance races. "The Big Cat" has now bought into the Stewart team and aims to add F1 to its roll of honour.

Supertec, abandoned by Williams and BAR is now supplying Arrows in addition to Benetton.

The Arrows F1 engine is no more, to no one's great sorrow.

After Malaysia it is the USA's turn to jump back into the F1 cauldron with a race at the legendary Indy oval.

Joan Villadelprat, the ebullient Benetton sporting director is now in charge of sponsorship operations for Telefonica, which is associated among others with Minardi. He is replaced by Gordon Message.

Former Arrows team manager John Walton has become sporting director at Prost Grand Prix.

The mysterious Prince Malik Ibrahim had wanted to buy out the Arrows team. Turns out his eyes were bigger than his belly, or at least his wallet.

With the departure of Jackie Stewart comes the arrival of Neil Ressler, a Ford man appointed to run the Jaguar team.

On the engineer front, Malcolm Oastler replaces Adrian Reynard, who takes over research and development, as technical director at BAR. Sergio Rinland and Jackie Eckelaert joined Sauber. Tim Densham moved to Benetton.

COMING IN 2001

The Japanese marque Toyota had planned to enter F1 in 2002. The latest news is that they will bring that forward by a year.

Michelin comes back to Formula 1. Absent since 1984, the French company returns in 2001 with Williams and Toyota already on the books.

The return of Renault dominates the headlines.

THE CHARMS OF FORMULA

SPARE PARTS PRICE LIST

	£	US $
- Brake pads	90	140
- Brake disks	700	1076
- Steering wheel	18000	27692
- Seat	2000	3076
- Harness	1800	2770
- mirror	350	538
- Tyres*	812	1250
- Rim	400	615
- Suspension wishbone	1600	2461
- Damper	900	1384
- Pedal box	6000	9230
- Steering	8400	12923
- Hub and carrier	12600	19384
- Nose and front wing	11000	16923
- Rear wing	19000	29230
- Fuel cell	6500	10000
- Radiators (one set)	29000	44615
- Engine cover	7000	10769
- Flat bottom	6500	10 000
- Exhausts	4000	6153
- Front suspension	7500	11538
- Rear suspension	10000	15384
- Carbon tub	65000	100000
- Telemetry system	90000	138461
- Gearbox (titanium)*	240000	369230
- Clutch	5500	8461
- Electronic control unit	3500	5384
- Black box (the team's)	3000	4615
- Telemetry radio	500	770
- Wiring	400	615
- Engine - "customer"	90000	138461
- Engine - "works"	400000	615384

* Transmission is part of gearbox
* The cost of a "works" engine is purely symbolic as it is impossible to establish an accurate figure for a major manufacturer's research and development budget.

FORMULA I AND MONEY

A driver's fireproof race suit costs around ¿1000. Depending on the status of the team, a driver will use between 10 and 20 a year, often to meet the different requirements regarding tobacco advertising.
The mechanics involved in refuelling during the race will use two per year (30 to 40 people per team.)
A pair of race boots costs around ¿65.
A driver gets through about 10 pairs a year.
He will also work his way through 20 pairs of gloves at ¿30 pounds each.
When Ayrton Senna joined McLaren in 1988, he had his favourite pair of gloves. They were so worn and full of holes that most of the fingers

FORMULA I IN FIGURES

of the right hand glove were held together with black tape.

A complete set of flameproof underwear costs, 50 and a driver will use 20 sets a year.

Today, a war rages between suppliers. In the past, the top teams reached agreements which saw them supplied free of charge, while the less well off teams had to pay. Today, these suppliers have become sponsors of the teams. To be associated with a prestigious marque like Ferrari or McLaren does not come cheap. And the demands for product are continually increasing.
The better known drivers negotiate their own lucrative contracts to wear a particular brand of overall, gloves or helmet. A racing helmet costs around ¿1300 and weighs only 1300 grammes. Drivers use between 6 and 20 per year. For example, Bell bring a new helmet to every race for Michael Schumacher. On the back of each

* Tyre supplier Bridgestone enjoys a monopoly in F1 and bills tyres by the set of four rather than individually. (5000 dollars)

one is the flag of that nation and the date. Bell, Arai and Bieffe are the three main suppliers and they send someone to every race to look after and maintain their product.

A visor costs 40 and the drivers get through one a day. The visors are fitted with tear-off strips which protect it and are torn off as when they get dirty during a race. A driver will use 3 per race and 10 over the whole weekend.

DRIVERS SALARIES IN 2000

Formula 1 is still a long way off the situation in the USA, where salaries of drivers in Cart, IRL and Nascar are readily available to the nearest dollar. There is no such openness in grand prix racing. They just have a different mentality on the other side of the Atlantic. On top of that, paranoia reins in the F1 paddock.

The teams, hide, cover and disguise their cars and equipment as they live with a great big persecution complex. Engineers hang around the garages of rival teams with furtive expressions as they try and spot what is going on.

Despite this law of silence, rumours still circulate, be they about the drivers' salaries or the teams' budgets.

The figures are by necessity estimates, which when gathered together allow one to draw up a pecking order for driver salaries.

Today, one thing is certain. Michael Schumacher, who has been struggling for years to clinch that third title, is the best paid sportsman in the world. He is reckoned to earn around ‚30 million.

He beats NBA basketball's Shaquille O'Neal (29.5) the boxers Oscar De La Hoya (28) Mike Tyson (25) and golf's Tiger Woods (24.)
Sales from the "Michael Schumacher Collection" available through mail order from a 100 page catalogue are reckoned to bring in at least half his money.

	£	US $
- M. Schumacher	30000000	46150000
- J. Villeneuve	7800000	12000000
- M. Häkkinen	6500000	10000000
- E. Irvine	6500000	10000000
- R. Schumacher	5200000	8000000
- H.H. Frentzen	3900000	6000000
- R. Barrichello	3250000	5000000
- J. Alesi	2600000	4000000
- J. Herbert	2600000	4000000
- D. Coulthard	1950000	3000000
- G. Fisichella	1950000	3000000
- M. Salo	1950000	3000000
- A. Wurz	1625000	2500000
- P. Diniz	1300000	2000000
- R. Zonta	1300000	2000000
- J. Trulli	1300000	2000000

etc...

If you look at French driver Jean Alesi, on ‚2.6 million, he fares badly when compared to his football playing fellow countrymen, Nicolas Anelka (5.6million) and Zinedine Zidane (2.9.)

On a European level, behind Michael Schumacher, we find the Russian NHL hockey player Sergei Fedorov on ‚23 million, the British boxers Lennox Lewis (17.5) and Prince Naseem Hamed (12) and the Russian tennis player, Anna Kournikova (8 million.)

F1 TEAM BUDGETS IN 2000

While it is possible to piece together more or less accurately a picture of the drivers' incomes, through indiscretions and "Radio Paddock" gossip, getting a true idea of a team's budget is much harder as this is always a closely guarded secret.

With the unprecedented arrival of so many major manufacturers, the teams' total budgets are constantly and rapidly increasing.

The scale of their investment depends on their level of ambition.

For example, Mercedes, BMW and Honda are investing heavily for success in the short to medium term.

The DaimlerChrysler group of which Mercedes is a part, has just bought 40% of the shares in TAG McLaren. This investment, whose cost is naturally confidential, means it cannot stop trying. In Formula 1, one cannot rest on one's laurels.

One always has to put more in. How can one calculate the value, on top of the traditional partnership, the value of the supply of personal and equipment or the cost of research and development? Research departments concentrate in part or entirely on the evolutions of the future or on improving engines. As the competition hots up, the effort required is phenomenal. For the past few years, McLaren-Mercedes and Ferrari have dominated the sport. It comes as no surprise that they have the biggest budgets. Ferrari won the constructors' title in 1999 and it now must win the drivers' crown, the more prestigious of the two by a long way.

In order to achieve this, it's global budget, with help from partners Fiat, Philip Morris, Shell and others will put at the disposal of the legendary team, a sum of around 460 million dollars.

Of course one has to recognise that Ferrari produces its own engines. The competition is so tough that it takes ever more money to stay on

top. McLaren, aided by Mercedes and its sponsors, must dispose of a similar budget.

Here is one example of the lengths these two teams go to in their efforts to win. Both of them use a satellite which allows them to transmit to the factory, in real time, all the data acquired by the car. That way, thousands of pieces of information can be immediately analysed by engineers who are not at the event, but are working back at base on computers which cannot be transported.

In just a short space of time, Formula 1 has reached the cutting edge of technology. It is pushing back the boundaries and that does not come cheap.

Behind these two giants of the sport, the rest are marshalling their forces to catch up.

As far as the team pecking order goes, behind these two colossi, first off we must have BAR, bolstered by the arrival of Honda. Then comes Williams, which has tied its future in with BMW. Both these teams must have in the region of 80 million each.

Outside this impressive quartet, Eddie Jordan deserves the merit award. With a decidedly smaller budget, he led the assault last year and intends doing the same again this time. The cunning Irishman made the most of his excellent results to improve his standing. It is said he might have got his hands on 60 million; a figure which should also apply to Jaguar who now have Ford's money to play with, now the American company has bought out Stewart. Then we have Benetton, Prost and Sauber in the middle of the pack, with probably around 40 million apiece. Arrows, who had to smash open the piggy-bank to pay for Supertec engines and Minardi, both survive on around 30 million.

These minnows somehow survive on one tenth of what is spent by Ferrari and McLaren. That is something to be proud of, because despite the financial difference, the gap on the stopwatch is not so big. The last two teams spend around

40% of their hard-earned budget on buying and maintaining engines.

While Arrows can consider its move justified with the fact it is using a competitive Supertec engine, what can one say about Minardi? The pleasant and charismatic little Italian outfit is spending 20 million dollars on a 1998 Ford engine, which has around 100 ps less than the opposition.

Television rights are controlled by FOA - the Formula One Association. It pays back some of this money to the teams. In the past the amount depended on results. More recently, this money has been split equally between the teams. For the smaller outfits, this is manna from heaven, representing as much as 30% of their total budgets.

HOW IS A FORMULA 1 BUDGET SPENT?

The engine is of course the most important expense for the teams who do not get a free supply. For a middle order team, facing the world alone, this is how the budget is broken down:

- Engine	30 %
- Salaries *	16 %
- Driver salaries	15 %
- Parts and materials	15 %
- Amortising	7 %
- General expense	7 %
- Travel	6 %
- Testing	4 %

*Employment costs are much higher in France, Switzerland and Italy than they are in the UK and this difference in the tax structures makes a big difference to costs.

For the races outside Europe, finishing in the top ten in the constructors' world championship carries with it the right to a special concession from FOA.

These ten teams get free transport for 10 tonnes of freight and two cars. It is a hotly contested right.

All the teams send at least the amount offered free of charge. The cost of shipping is 20 dollars per kilo.

THE MCLAREN MERCEDES TEAM IN FIGURES

The McLaren team has long been the reference point when it comes to organisation. Here it lets us into its secrets:

McLaren sends between 60 and 100 people to every grand prix, in the following way:
- McLaren 60 to 65 for European races
50 to 55 for "flyaways"
- Mercedes 20 to 25 for European races
15 to 20 for "flyaways."

The race team comprises a technical director, a chief race engineer, a chief mechanic, a computer expert, a race strategist, a track engineer, an assistant engineer, a fabrication engineer, a data analyst, twelve mechanics per driver, a carbon specialist, a transport chief, two people for the tyres, a fuel expert and an assistant, a spares man, a team coordinator, an audiovisual technician and two engineers for the radio system.

The test team has a similar set up.

The McLaren team transports around 24 tonnes of material, including three complete cars which weigh around 600 kilos each.
It used around 1000 commercial flights in 1999 for testing, races and business travel.
It required 1450 hotel rooms for the team and its partners during the season and 780 for private testing.

The McLarens did around 36500 kilometres of testing during the 1999 season.

In the races, they did around 21,000 kilometres.

McLaren-Mercedes take eight engines and four gearboxes to each race.

In 1999, it got through 56500 litres of fuel.

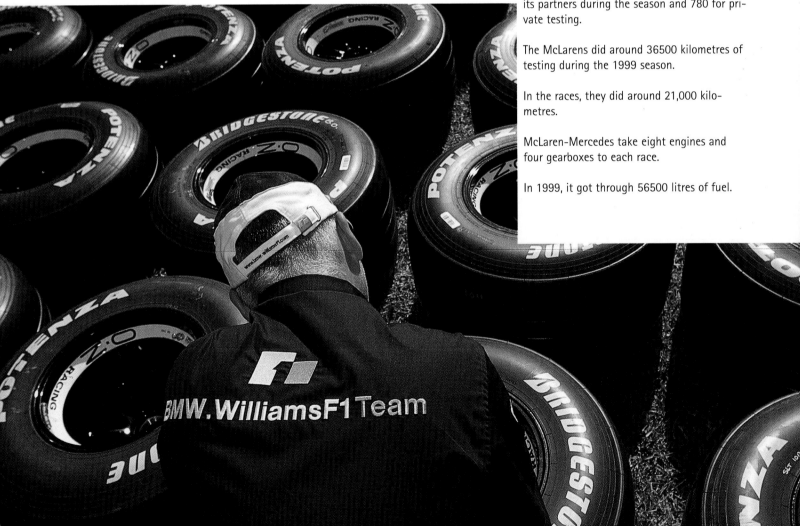

In an average race, there will be 2500 gearchanges. This number can be higher in Montreal and lower in Hockenheim.

The drivers lose around two kilos in weight and two litres of fluid during a race.

A driver's neck takes a pasting during a race. Centrifugal and longitudinal forces during braking and cornering and acceleration through corners causes this. The force can be as high as 5G.

A driver's neck can support five times the weight of his head and helmet, or around 25 kilos. Imagine 25 bags of sugar tied to your head!

FORMULA 1 AND TELEVISION

FIA has recently published television broadcast statistics

	Total number of viewers*	Total number of minutes broadcast	Total number of broadcasts	Total number of countries taking broadcasts
1999	57 754 361 716	1 338 272	68 782	206
1998	55 238 397 676	1 275 235	72 637	209
1997	50 732 645 052	1 061 049	52 970	193
1996	40 992 557 185	1 631 304	52 588	202
1995	45 047 983 000	1 586 073	50 912	201

* The number of viewers indicates how many times a programme has been watched, not necessarily by different people. So if a person watches four different programmes, it is counted as four viewers.

From this mass of figures one can see an increase of 2.5 billion over 1998. However, there is a slight drop in the number of countries broadcasting.

THE MAGIOR SPONSORS IN FORMULA 1
Living out the cash injected by the manufacturers here is a chart of the big spenders in Formula 1

	US$	£
- Lucky Strike (BAR)	75 millions	49,5 millions
- Marlboro (Ferrari)	65 millions	42,9 millions
- West (McLaren)	37 millions	24,4 millions
- Compaq (Williams)	35 millions	23,1 millions
- Orange (Arrows)	35 millions	23,1 millions
- Petronas (Sauber)	33 millions	21,8 millions
- Benson (Jordan)	30 millions	19,8 millions
- Mild Seven (Benetton)	30 millions	19,8 millions
- Gauloises (Prost)	22 millions	14,5 millions
- Mobil (McLaren)	22 millions	14,5 millions
- HSBC (Jaguar)	20 millions	13,2 millions
- Yahoo! (Prost)	20 millions	13,2 millions
- Shell (Ferrari)	20 millions	13,2 millions
- Telefonica (Minardi)	20 millions	13,2 millions

Mika Häkkinen the man to beat

Since his win in the 1997 European Grand Prix, Mika Hakkinen, the man who was seriously injured in Australia in 1995 and was regularly the victim of bad luck, has now become a new man. Indeed, his success in Jerez seemed to flick a switch to start the rest of his career.

The return to the top for McLaren after a difficult start with Mercedes signalled the start of a rocket-like progression for the Finnish driver which led to glory. In 1998, despite a Michael Schumacher still very much on top of his form, Mika Hakkinen dominated with brio and panache. He knew how to stand up to the pressure without cracking. He took his title at the very last race of the championship at Suzuka. Last year, it was in Japan again, this time defeating Eddie Irvine after Michael Schumacher had been sidelined through injury. Success is finally smiling on him. He now has back to back world titles to his name. "At the end of that 1999 season, I wondered if I would be able to motivate myself to do it again in 2000. Then after a good winter break, I started to think about the possibility of a third title. Today, I am absolutely up for it. My "sisu" or fighting spirit is very strong. I am very hopeful."

Suntanned, relaxed and rested after almost three months holiday with his wife Erja, Mika Hakkinen came back stronger than ever. It will take something special to derail the Hakkinen-McLaren express. He is determined to make his mark on history. If he secured his hat-trick of titles, he would be well on the way to matching Juan Manuel Fangio's achievement of four world championship crowns in a row.

A

Adams Philippe (2)	No longer competing
Alboreto Michele 194	Endurance (Audi)
Alesi Jean (167)	Formule 1 (Prost)
Alliot Philippe (109)	Rallye Raid Dakar-Cairo (Mercedes)
Andretti Michael (13)	Formule Cart in USA (Newman-Haas)
Apicella Marco (1)	Endurance (Porsche GT3)

Michele Alboreto

B

Badoer Luca (51)	Test driver Ferrari
Bailey Julian (7)	Endurance GT (Lister)
Barbazza Fabrizio (8)	No longer competing
Barilla Paolo (15)	Gone back to working in business (Barilla pasta)
Barrichello Rubens (113)	Formule 1 (Ferrari)
Belmondo Paul (7)	Owner and driver of Dodge Viper team in endurance
Beretta Olivier (10)	Endurance (Chrysler Viper)
Berger Gerhard (210)	BMW motor sport boss
Bernard Eric (45)	Endurance (Cadillac DAMS)
Blundell Mark (61)	Formule Cart in USA (Pac-West)
Boullion Jean-Christophe (11)	No longer competing
Boutsen Thierry (163)	Sale and maintenance of private planes
Brabham David (24)	Endurance (Panoz)
Brundle Martin (158)	TV consultant

WHAT HAS BECOME OF THEM

Michael Andretti

C

Caffi Alex (56)	Endurance (Ferrari 333 SP)
Capelli Ivan (93)	Endurance N- GT (Ferrari 360 M)
De Cesaris Andrea (208)	No longer competing
Chiesa Andrea (3)	Working as TV consultant in Switzerland
Comas Erik (59)	Endurance GT in Japon (Nissan)
Coulthard David (90)	Formule 1 (McLaren)

D

Dalmas Yannick (24)	No longer competing
De la Rosa Pedro (16)	Formule 1 (Arrows)
Deletraz Jean-Denis (3)	Endurance N-GT (Ferrari 360 M)
Diniz Pedro (82)	Formule 1 (Sauber)
Donnelly Martin (14)	F3 team owner in UK

Eric Bernard

Mark Blundell

F

Fisichella Giancarlo (57)   Formule 1 (Benetton)
Fittipaldi Christian (40)   Formule Cart in USA (Newman-Haas)
Foitek Gregor (7)   In business
Fontana Norberto (4)   Formule Cart in USA (Della Penna)
Frentzen Heinz-Harald (97)   Formule 1 (Jordan)

G

Gachot Bertrand (47)   Business
Giacomelli Bruno (69)   Business
Gounon Jean-Marc (9)   Endurance in USA (BMW Schnitzer)
Grouillard Olivier (41)   Le Mans (Courage-Peugeot)
Gugelmin Maurizio (74)   Formule Cart (Pac-West)

Damon Hill

H

Häkkinen Mika (128)   Formule 1 (McLaren)
Herbert Johnny (145)   Formule 1 (Jaguar)
Hill Damon (116)   Presents TV programme in UK

IJK

Inoue Taki (18)   Endurance (Ferrari F 355)
Irvine Eddie (97)   Formule 1 (Jaguar)
Johansson Stefan (79)   Endurance (Reynard) and IRL team boss in USA
Katayama Ukyo (95)   Endurance GT in Japan (Nissan)

G. Fisichella, P. De la Rosa and J. Trulli

L

Lagorce Franck (2)   Endurance (Cadillac)
Lammers Jan (23)   Endurance (Lola)
Lamy Pedro (32)   DTM touring care in Germany (Mercedes)
Larini Nicola (49)   Endurance in USA (Lola and Riley-Scott and Touring cars (Alfa Romeo)
Lavaggi Giovanni (7)   No longer competing
Lehto Giovanni   Endurance in USA (BMW Schnitzer)

M

Mansell Nigel (187)   Golf club owner and businessman
Magnussen Jan (24)   Endurance (Panoz)
Marques Tarso (11)   No longer competing
Martini Pierluigi (119)   Endurance (Lola Rafanelli)
Modena Stefano (70)   DTM touring cars in Germany (Opel)
Montermini Andrea (21)   No longer competing
Morbidelli Gianni (67)   DTM in Germany (Volvo)
Moreno Roberto(42)   Formule Cart in USA (Patrick Racing)

Nigel Mansell

N

Nakajima Satoru (74) Boss of "Nakajima Planning", working in F3 and F3000 in Japan
Nakano Shinji (33) Formule Cart in USA (Walker Racing)
Nannini Alessandro (77) In business
Naspetti Emmanuelle (6) Endurance (Porsche GT3)
Noda Hideki (3) No longer competing

Olivier Panis

P

Panis Olivier (91) Formula 1 (McLaren test and reserve driver)
Papis Massimo (7) Endurance (Riley & Scott) and CART in USA (Rahal)
Patrese Ricardo (256) In business
Piquet Nelson (204) Businessman and some endurance racing in Brazil
Pirro Emmanuelle (37) Endurance (Audi)
Prost Alain (199) F1 team owner (Prost GP)

R

Ratzenberger Roland (1) Died at Imola in 1994
Rosset Ricardo (32) In business

Alain Prost

S

Salo Mika (78) Formule 1 (Sauber)
Schiatarella Domenico (6) Endurance (Ferrari)
Schneider Bernd (9) DTM touring cars in Germany (Mercedes)
Schumacher Michael Formule 1 (Ferrari 333 SP)
Schumacher Ralf (49) Formule 1 (Williams)
Senna Ayrton (161) Died at Imola in 1994
Suzuki Aguri (64) Endurance GT in Japan (Honda)

Michael Schumacher

T

Takagi Toranosuke (32) Formule 3000 in Japan (Nakajima)
Tarquini Gabriele (38) British Touring Cars (Honda)
Tuero Esteban (16) Touring Cars in Argentina
Trulli Jarno (46) Formule 1 (Jordan)

Ayrton Senna

V

Van de Poele Eric (5) — Endurance (Cadillac)
Verstappen Jos (57) — Formule 1 (Arrows)
Villeneuve Jacques (65) — Formule 1 (BAR)

W

Warwick Derek (147) — In business
Wendlinger Karl (41) — Endurance GT (Chrysler Viper)
Wurz Alexander (35) — Formule 1 (Benetton)

Z

Zanardi Alex (41) — No longer competing
Zonta Ricardo (16) — Formule 1 (BAR)

NOTE: The number of grands prix entered is shown in brackets after each name.
A grand prix driver is one who has actually started a grand prix.

Jacques Villeneuve

Ricardo Zonta

THE LAUNCH HIT PARADE

Back in the Seventies, some of the tobacco companies would organise small, almost private presentations to launch a new car in their colours. In the Eighties, Ferrari turned this into a virtual ritual. Each new F1 car was presented with great pomp on the legendary Fiorano race track. Lotus and Benetton soon followed suit. The other teams preferred the low key approach at Silverstone or Le Castellet, where they would run their new cars without any fuss.

These days, the new car presentation, prior to the start of the season, has become a major media event, with each team desperately trying to out-do the other.

In 1996, Benetton and its partner Renault, chartered several planes to fly the press down to Sicily, where it unveiled its Formula 1 car in the ancient theatre at Taormina, under the guidance of the Emperor Briatore!

Nothing quite as spectacular takes place these days, but everyone has some sort of launch. This year the exception was Arrows, who were caught out by the very late arrival of a major sponsor. A posse of journalists and photographers charge across Europe from one launch to the next and this cynical jurists came up with a hit parade of the 2000 presentations. Here are the results. There were eight points to be judged on: the originality of the venue, the effort in finding it, the accessibility for photos and how easy it was to work, the general organisation, the press conference, the press kit and last but definitely not least, the quality of the buffet!

- 1st Benetton: The B200 was presented on 17th January in front of the Catalunya Art Museum in Montjuich Park, which overlooks the centre of Barcelona. Immaculate organisation.
(127 points, 15.87/20)

- 2nd McLaren: The MP4/15 was unveiled on 3rd February at Jerez circuit in the team's portable VIP hospitality area. There was nothing original about it but it was perfectly organised, as one expects from this team.
(123 points, 15.37/20)

- 3rd The F1 2000 made its debut on 7th February, in an enormous marquee in the heart of the Ferrari road car factory. Classical and classy and well organised.
(121 points, 15.12/20)

- 4th Jaguar: The Jaguar R1 was revealed at Lords Cricket Ground in a temporary structure. A well run event in the world centre for Cricket.
(105 points, 13.12/20)

- 5th BAR: The BAR 002 was shown on 24th January at the Queen Elizabeth II Conference Centre in London. It was low key, but well organised.
(100 points, 12.50/20)

- 6th Minardi: The Minardi M02 was launched on 16th February at the Guggenheim Museum in Bilbao. After a press conference held in a marquee, the car was unveiled outside, at night and in the pouring rain. A shame that the building's impressive facade was hidden in the darkness.
(97 points, 12.12/20)

- 7th Prost: The Prost AP03 was shown on 1st February at the Barcelona circuit in a large marquee. Well organised, except that the major players were not well lit on stage.
(96 points, 12/20)

- 8th Jordan: The Jordan EJ-10 was unveiled on 31st January at London's Theatre Royal, Drury Lane. While the presentation was good and Eddie Jordan was in fine form, it was hard to take photos and the venue was too cramped.
(93 points, 11.62/20)

- 9th Sauber: The Sauber C19 was revealed on 2nd February at 8 pm in the Hallenstadion in Zurich. A press presentation went off perfectly in the afternoon. The Swiss team decided to launch in front of the general public, who are usually not admitted to this type of event.
Over 8000 people paid to get in and things got chaotic as they all wanted to get at the car.
(82 points, 10.25/20)

- 10th Williams: For the past two years, Williams appears to deliberately choose a date when another team is launching, thus forcing the media to make a choice.
After a show in Munich on 10th January to show off the Williams-BMW livery, the real presentation took place at the Barcelona circuit on 24th January. The photo call, in a corner of the garage, was not worthy of this team's ambitions.
(78 points, 9.75/20)

Friday 27th August 1999 at the Belgian Grand Prix and Alain Prost is in the paddock at Spa, about to announce to the assembled media huddle the names of his drivers for the following season. Jean Alesi would be partnered by the yung German, Nick Heidfeld.

It was an embarrassing moment for Olivier Panis. At this point in the season, there are not too many drives going begging. He is in with a chance at Arrows. But the drive requires a huge pot of gold to secure it and the price is too high. Then, during the summer, Keke Rosberg, a former world champion and Mika Hakkinen's manager agreed to take Olivier Panis under his wing.

Between Malaysia and Japan, the last two grands prix of the season, while the rest of the Formula 1 world is lounging around under tropical skies, Olivier Panis headed back to France and did two days testing for McLaren at Magny-Cours.

Re-motivated and on a high after this experience, followed by three days rest and relaxation at the Sherating Club Med, the French driver said goodbye to the Prost team in fine style. Sixth on the grid, he made a great start and moved up to third, behind Hakkinen and Schumacher. He had no trouble keeping the pack at bay. Let down by his gearbox after his first pit stop on lap 20, he had to retire after this

Olivier had the choice.

His decision was that of a wise man. He had at least two possibilities to be on the grid at Melbourne this year, but what position would he have been in? Arrows is an experienced team, but it would not have given him the chance to get to the front. Neither did he want to be a guinea pig for Williams while it went through its learning phase with the new BMW engine. Frank Williams was unable to offer him a long term contract.

Olivier is clear about what he wants. "I do not want to be in F1 just to take part. After six years, I want to fight for wins and for the championship. It is another take on F1. I have given myself one year to get a drive with a good team. I do not want to miss out on this chance of driving for the best team for my future career."

Right from the start of testing in December, at the wheel of one of the very best cars, Panis rediscovered the simple pleasure of driving. He also found a team which listened to him and the happiness which came from driving the car which had just won the championship for the best team of all.

"It is very exciting driving the car which has just won the championship. The McLaren is no easier to drive than the others, but it is one and a half seconds quicker."

ning, but I will tell myself I played a small part in the victory."

Olivier Panis had been looking for a trampoline to relaunch his career. For sure, he would have had a knot in his stomach when the red lights went out on the grid in Melbourne, to signal the season had started without him. "But I have no regrets as I have chosen the right solution."

Through these images, Olivier Panis talks us through his new life as McLaren's third driver, during a three day test session at Jerez, in the south of Spain in December 1999, just a few days after signing his contract.

Photo 1. "Monday, 13th December at one o'clock. I leave Grenoble for a direct flight to Jerez in a Beech 100."

A NEW LIFE FOR OLIVIER PANIS

surprising performance.

It is the end of an era. Olivier Panis made his F1 debut with Ligier in 1994. He stayed faithful to the "Blues" even after Prost picked up the reins in 1997. He contested 91 grands prix, won at Monaco in 1996, finished second three times and scored one third place. He scored 56 points.

On several occasions he resisted the siren call of, among others Eddie Jordan, to remain faithful to the French team.

Last November, the month when testing is banned, it was all go and the Olivier's mobile never stopped ringing.

Frank Williams wants to split from Zanardi. He pushes hard to get Panis to partner Ralf Schumacher. Arrows boss Tom Walkinshaw is also shopping around once more. During this time, in early December, Olivier drives two more test sessions for McLaren at Barcelona and then in Jerez. On 2nd December 1999, a McLaren press release announces that Olivier Panis has been employed as the team's third driver. Ron Dennis insists on the time "third driver" and not "test driver." This means the Frenchman can step in if needed.

"I know how awful it is to have an accident and I would not want to be given a drive under these circumstances."

One should always treat winter testing times with a pinch of salt. The teams are working on different programmes. Some are looking for endurance, others are tyre testing, while some are seeking outright performance. Even taking all these factors into consideration, Olivier's times were excellent.

His confidence came back very quickly. "The spiral of defeat," as Alain Prost called it, is now a thing of the past. Wound up once again, the real Panis reappeared, happier than we had seen him for a long time. He is really motivated now, smiling and ready for anything.

This year, he will do around 15,000 kilometres of testing with an average of eight days testing per month. "I was lucky enough to develop the new Mercedes engine for one and a half months. Mika and David are full of confidence in my work. They are happy to rely on someone with a lot of experience."

He turned down a drive in the German DTM Touring Car programme with the Mercedes team run by his manager Keke Rosberg, in order to concentrate 100% on his job as the third McLaren driver.

"If I had tackled the DTM, I would have wanted to win. Well, with my F1 testing schedule and the fact the team wants me to attend most of the grands prix, I would not have had the time for the Touring Cars. It might be a bit difficult watching Mika or David win-

Photos 2 and 3. "The flight lasts four hours. I have time to have a good look around and even take the controls of the aircraft!"

Photo 4. "After a good night's rest, the day starts early. The first briefing takes place at 7.45. With the engineers, we fix the programme for the day. This meeting lasts around 20 minutes. Then I go to the garage. It is 8.30."

Photo 5. "Sat in the McLaren, I wait for the green light at 9 o'clock to leave the pit lane."

Photo 6. "At 9 o'clock precisely, when the sun is already high in the Andalusian sky, I go out for an installation lap. Then the mechanics check this test car over. It is actually the 1999 car with the 2000 engine."

Photo 7. "Between each run, or every 3 to 4 laps, I get out of the car and we analyse what it has done, the handling of the car and especially the effect of the engine modifications."

Photo 8. "Sometimes the stops are long and you have to learn to be patient!"

Photo 9. "Back on track around 11.30, I try some new settings."

Photo 10. "After an unscheduled briefing at lunchtime, I am ready for action again."

Photos 11, 12, 13. "During this test session, I only did 15 laps on the first day, 55 on the second and 80 on the third; equivalent to around 600 kilometres. That's the same as two grands prix. I was pleased to set the fastest time on the Wednesday."

Photos 14, 15. "We make the most of the last few minutes before the track is closed to round off our development programme. It is almost six pm.

Photos 16, 17, 18. "Satisfied with a job well done, I join David Coulthard in the truck. After getting changed, we tackle the evening briefing in the motorhome. It lasts about two hours. We are in permanent contact with the factory, via satellite link."

Photo 19. "This test session is now over. I rush to the plane and its waiting crew."

Photo 20, 21. "I had no time to eat at lunchtime. I tuck into a nice sandwich before a welcome sleep. We will arrive in Grenoble after midnight, having encountered strong head winds.
I join my family for the weekend, before heading to the McLaren factory in Woking on Monday for a two day simulation session."

HERE ARE THE ANSWERS TO SOME OF THE QUESTIONS YOU MIGHT HAVE THOUGHT OF ASKING...

THE SHORTEST CIRCUIT TO HAVE STAGED A G.P.?
Long Beach in the USA in 1976 (3,220 km).

THE LONGEST CIRCUIT TO HAVE STAGED A G.P.?
Pescara in Italy in 1957 (25,838 km).

THE LONGEST DISTANCE RUN IN A G.P.?
500 miles in Indianapolis (805 km).

THE BIGGEST NUMBER OF STARTERS IN A G.P. ?
34 in Germany in 1953 (Nürburgring).

THE SMALLEST NUMBER OF STARTERS IN A G.P. ?
13 in Spain in 1968 (Jarama).

THE BIGGEST NUMBER OF FINISHERS IN A G.P. ?
22 in the British GP of 1952 (Silverstone).

THE SMALLEST NUMBER OF FINISHERS IN A G.P. ?
4 at Monaco in 1966.

THE CIRCUIT WHICH HAS STAGED THE MOST G.P. ?
Monza, 49 times.

THE GREATEST NUMBER OF G.P. WINS?
Alain Prost (51 wins).

THE GREATEST NUMBER OF G.P. SECOND PLACE FINISHES?
Alain Prost (35).

THE GREATEST NUMBER OF G.P. THIRD PLACE FINISHES?
Gerhard Berger (21).

THE GREATEST NUMBER OF G.P. PODIUM FINISHES ?
Alain Prost (106).

THE GREATEST NUMBER OF POINTS SCORED?
Alain Prost (798,5 points).

DID YOU KNOW?

THE LONGEST TIME TAKEN TO RUN A G.P.?
Indianapolis in 1951 (3h 57'38").

THE SHORTEST G.P. IN TERMS OF DISTANCE?
Adelaïde in Australia in 1991 (53 km).

THE SHORTEST G.P. IN 2000 IN TERMS OF DISTANCE?
Monaco, 263,484 km.

THE LONGEST G.P. IN 2000 IN TERMS OF DISTANCE?
Suzuka in Japon (310,476 km).

NUMBER OF COUNTRIES WHICH HAS ORGANISED A G.P.?
24.

NUMBER OF CIRCUITS USED TO HOST A G.P.?
59.

FASTEST AVERAGE QUALIFYING SPEED?
Keke Rosberg at the 1985 British GP (258,984 km/h).

THE HIGHEST AVERAGE RACE SPEED IN A G.P.?
Damon Hill at Monza in 1993 (249,835 km/h).

THE BIGGEST WINNING MARGIN AT THE END OF A GRAND PRIX.?
2 laps in Spain in 1969, between Stewart and McLaren et in Australia in1995 between Hill and Panis.

THE SMALLEST WINNING MARGIN?
10 thousandths of a second between Gethin and Peterson at Monza in 1971.

THE YOUNGEST DRIVER TO HAVE STARTED A G.P. ?
Mike Thackwell, 19 years old (Canada 1980).

THE OLDEST DRIVER TO HAVE STARTED A G.P. ?
Louis Chiron, 55 years old (Monaco 1955).

THE YOUNGEST WINNER OF A G.P. ?
Troy Ruttmann, 22 years old (Indianapolis 1952).

THE OLDEST WINNER OF A G.P. ?
Luigi Fagioli, 53 years old (France 1951).

THE YOUNGEST WORLD CHAMPION?
Emerson Fittipaldi, 25 years old in 1972.

THE OLDEST WORLD CHAMPION?
Juan Manuel Fangio 46 years old in 1957.

THE GREATEST NUMBER OF CHAMPIONSHIP TITLES ?
5 (Juan Manuel Fangio).

THE BIGGEST WINNING MARGIN IN A WORLD CHAMPION-SHIP?
52 points separated Nigel Mansell and Ricardo Patrese in 1992.

THE SMALLEST WINNING MARGIN IN A WORLD CHAMPION-SHIP?
Half a point separated Niki Lauda and Alain Prost in 1984.

THE GREAT NUMBER OF GRANDS PRIX CONTESTED?
Ricardo Patrese (256).

THE GREATEST NUMBER OF POINTS SCORED IN ONE SEASON?
Nigel Mansell in 1992 (108 points).

THE GREATEST NUMBER OF WINS IN ONE SEASON?
Nigel Mansell in 1992 and Michael Schumacher in 1995 (9 wins).

THE GREATEST NUMBER OF WINS IN THE SAME G.P.?
Ayrton Senna in Monaco, Alain Prost in Brazil et in France (6 times).

THE GREATEST NUMBER OF SUCCESSIVE WINS?
Alberto Ascari in 1952 and 53 (9 wins).

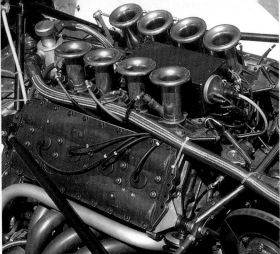

THE HIGHEST NUMBER OF KILOMETRES RUN IN THE LEAD BY A DRIVER?
Ayrton Senna (13 469 Km).

THE HIGHEST NUMBER OF POLE POSITIONS?
Ayrton Senna (65 pole positions).

THE HIGHEST NUMBER OF POLE POSITIONS IN A SEASON?
Nigel Mansell en 1992 (14 pole positions).

THE HIGHEST NUMBER OF RACE FASTEST LAPS?
Alain Prost (41).

THE HIGHEST NUMBER OF RACE FASTEST LAPS PER SEASON?
Nigel Mansell in 1992 (8).

THE HIGHEST NUMBER OF WINS PER NATION?
182 with 17 drivers for Great Britain.

THE GREATEST NUMBER OF GP WINS FOR A TEAM?
Ferrari (125 victoires).

THE GREATEST NUMBER OF CONSTRUCTORS' TITLES?
Williams and Ferrari (9 titles).

THE HIGHEST NUMBER OF POINTS SCORED IN A SEASON?
McLaren in 1988 (199 points).

THE HIGHEST TOTAL NUMBER OF POINTS SCORED BETWEEN 1950 AND 1999?
Ferrari (22390 points).

THE HIGHEST NUMBER OF WINS SCORED IN A SEASON BY A TITLE WINNING DRIVER?
Nigel Mansell in 1992 and Michael Schumacher in 1995 (9 wins).

THE LOWEST NUMBER OF WINS SCORED IN A SEASON BY A TITLE WINNING DRIVER?
Mike Hawthorn in 1958 and Keke Rosberg in 1982 (1 win).

THE HIGHEST NUMBER OF ONE-TWO FINISHES?
41 (Ferrari).

THE HIGHEST NUMBER OF ONE-TWO FINISHES IN A SEASON?
McLaren in 1988 (10).

THE HIGHEST NUMBER OF POLE POSITIONS FOR A CONSTRUCTOR?
Ferrari (127).

THE HIGHEST NUMBER OF POLE POSITIONS FOR A CONSTRUCTOR IN ONE SEASON?
Mclaren in 1988 and 89 and Williams in 1992 and 93 (15 pole positions).

THE GREATEST NUMBER OF WINS AT ONE CIRCUIT?
Ferrari in Italie at Monza (12).

THE HIGHEST NUMBER OF WINS FOR AN ENGINE?
Ford (175).

THE HIGHEST NUMBER OF WINS FOR AN ENGINE IN ONE SEASON?
Renault in 1995 (16 wins).

MOST POLES PER ENGINE IN A SEASON?
Renault in 1995 (16).

WHICH DRIVER HAS DRIVEN FOR THE GREATEST NUMBER OF TEAMS?
Andrea De Cesaris drove for 10 different team in 208 grands prix from 1980 to 1994.

WHICH DRIVERS HAVE BEEN TEAM MATES FOR THE LONGEST TIME?
Gerhard Berger and Jean Alesi (5 years, of which 3 at Ferrari and 2 with Benetton). They drove 77 GPs together.

THE ACCELERATION OF A FORMULA 1 CAR?

From 0 to 100 km/h	2,3 seconds.
From 0 to 160 km/h	3,6 seconds.
From 0 to 160 km/h to 0	6,6 seconds.

THE DATES FOR THE 2000 SEASON

12TH MARCH	AUSTRALIAN GRAND PRIX (MELBOURNE)
26TH MARCH	BRAZILIAN GRAND PRIX (SAO PAULO)
9TH APRIL	SAN MARINO GRAND PRIX (IMOLA)
23RD APRIL	BRITISH GRAND PRIX (SILVERSTONE)
7TH MAY	SPANISH GRAND PRIX (BARCELONA)
21ST MAY	EUROPEAN GRAND PRIX (NURBURGRING)
4TH JUNE	MONACO GRAND PRIX (MONTE-CARLO)
18TH JUNE	CANADIAN GRAND PRIX (MONTREAL)
2ND JULY	FRENCH GRAND PRIX (MAGNY COURS)
16TH JULY	AUSTRIAN GRAND PRIX (ZELTWEG)
30TH JULY	GERMAN GRAND PRIX (HOCKENHEIM)
13TH AUGUST	HUNGARIAN GRAND PRIX (BUDAPEST)
27TH AUGUST	BELGIAN GRAND PRIX (SPA-FRANCORCHAMPS)
10TH SEPTEMBER	ITALIAN GRAND PRIX (MONZA)
24TH SEPTEMBER	USA GRAND PRIX (INDIANAPOLIS)
8TH OCTOBER	JAPANESE GRAND PRIX (SUZUKA)
22ND OCTOBER	MALAYSIAN GRAND PRIX (KUALA LUMPUR)

THE GRANDS PRIX

AUSTRALIAN GRAND PRIX
SUNDAY 12TH MARCH 2000
MELBOURNE

1999 STATISTICS

START GRID:

1st	M. Häkkinen (McLaren-Mercedes)	1'30"462
2	D. Coulthard (McLaren-Mercedes)	1'30"946
3	M. Schumacher (Ferrari)	1'31"781
4	R. Barrichello (Stewart-Ford)	1'32"348
5	H.-H. Frentzen (Jordan-Mugen-Honda)	1'32"276
6	E. Irvine (Ferrari)	1'32"289

etc...

RACE RESULT:

1st	E. Irvine (Ferrari)	in 1h 35'01"659
2	H.-H Frentzen (Jordan-Mugen-Honda)	1"026
3	R. Schumacher (Williams-Supertec)	7"012
4	G. Fisichella (Benetton-Playlife)	33"418
5	R. Barrichello (Stewart-Ford)	54"697
6	P. De la Rosa (Arrows)	1'24"316
7	T. Takagi (Arrows)	1'26"288
8	M. Schumacher (Ferrari)	1 lap

FASTEST LAPS 1999:

M. Schumacher (Ferrari) : 1'32"112 at 207,256 km/h.

LAP RECORD:

H.-H. Frentzen (Williams-Renault) in 1997 : 1'30"585 at 210,710 km/h.

RACE HISTORY

1999 : E. Irvine (Ferrari)
1998 : M. Häkkinen (Mclaren)
1997 : D. Coulthard (McLaren)
1996 : D. Hill (Williams)
1995 : D. Hill (Williams)
1994 : N. Mansell (Williams)
1993 : A. Senna (McLaren)
1992 : R. Patrese (Williams)
1991 : A. Senna (McLaren)
1990 : N. Piquet (Benetton)
etc...

Alain Prost (1986 and 88), Ayrton Senna (1991 and 93) and Damon Hill (1995 eand 96) won two Australian GP. The first winner was Keke Rosberg (Williams) in 1985.

There have been 15 Australian Grands Prix.
Adelaïde : from 1985 to 1995.
Melbourne : from 1996.

Start :   14h00 local time, 04h00 in UK.
Distance : 58 laps of 5.316 km, a total of 308,328 km.
1999 : 118 000 spectators on Sunday.
Location : The circuit is situated to the south of Melbourne, less than 10 kilometres from the city centre. Nearest airport is Melbourne-Tullamarine, 21 kilometres north of the city.

This year, the Olympic Games take place in Sydney, Australia. Melbourne will find it hard to live up to that sort of excitement. It has hosted the opening round of the Formula One World Championship for five years now. The Australian Grand Prix is now a regular fixture, whereas the Olympics are a unique event. The last time the Olympic flame burned on Australian soil, it was in fact in Melbourne in 1956. However, the Albert Park Grand Prix grandstands will no doubt be full to bursting point for the first race of 2000.
The circuit which winds around a lake which is home to black and white swans, is not the most interesting in the world, but it has a certain charm. The event is impeccably organised and the Australians give it a warm welcome, making this long distance venue a very pleasant one.

MELBOURNE AS SEEN BY JARNO TRULLI :

"I have always liked the Melbourne circuit. The track is nothing special mind you, but it is not that easy to find the right lines. I like Australia and I feel comfortable there. I am more than happy to attend this race."

Address :
Albert Park Grand Prix Circuit,
220 Albert Road
South Melbourne, Australia
Tel : 00 61 3 92 58 71 00
Fax : 00 61 3 96 99 37 27

BRAZILIAN GRAND PRIX
INTERLAGOS
SUNDAY 26 MARCH 2000

Start : 13h00, 14h00 in Europe.
60 laps of 5.141 km or 308.289 km.
Attendance en 1999 : 120 000 spectators on Sunday.
Location: Silverstone circuit is 110 kilometres to the north west of London, 25 kilometres to the south east of Northampton and 45 kilometres from Oxford. The nearest airports are Birmingham (50 km) London Heathrow and Luton.

"The home of motor sport" is Silverstone's motto and so it is. Most of the Formula 1 teams are based within striking distance of the former Royal Air Force airfield. This year, FIA has made some radical changes to the traditional calendar. For decades, the British Grand Prix has been held in mid-July, the best time of the year with the most chance of sunshine and the least possibility of rain.
Last year, the wet races were thrilling and full of incident. Putting on this event in April, there is a much higher chance of the race taking place in the rain. The organisers tried in vain to swop dates with Austria, but the risk of snow in Styria meant this was a non-starter. No doubt Easter weekend in the English countryside will be very interesting. Especially if you are nice and warm at home in front of the television.

> **SILVERSTONE AS SEEN BY JARNO TRULLI :**
> "I don't want to think about it. It can rain here all the time even in summer, so what will it be like in April? It is not one of my favourite races, but the atmosphere is nice. It is a very demanding track technically. It is essential to have a good understanding of the circuit and of your car. This year, driving a Jordan, built outside the circuit gates, Heinz-Harald Frentzen and I will have a slight advantage over the others."

Address :
Autodromo Jose Carlos Pace
Av. Senador Teotonio Vilelia 261
Sao Paolo, Brazil.
Tel : 00 55 11 52 19 911
Fax : 00 55 11 24 24 494

1999 STATISTICS

START GRID:

1st	M. Häkkinen (McLaren-Mercedes)	1'16"568
2	D. Coulthard (McLaren-Mercedes)	1'16"715
3	M. Schumacher (Ferrari)	1'17"305
4	R. Barrichello (Stewart-Ford)	1'17"578
5	H.-H. Frentzen (Jordan-Mugen-Honda)	1'17"810
6	E. Irvine (Ferrari)	1'17"843

etc...

RACE RESULT:

1st	M. Häkkinen (McLaren-Mercedes) in 1h 36'03"785
		192,994 km/h
2	M.Schumacher (Ferrari)	4"925
3	H.-H. Frentzen (Jordan-Mugen-Honda)	1 lap
4	R. Schumacher (Williams-Supertec)	1 lap
5	E. Irvine (Ferrari)	1 lap
6	O. Panis (Prost-Peugeot)	1 lap
7.	A. Wurz (Benetton-Playlife)	2 laps
8	T. Takagi (Arrows)	3 laps
9	M. Gene (Minardi-Ford)	3 laps

FASTEST LAPS 1999:

M. Häkkinen (McLaren-Mercedes) :
1'18"448 at 196,961 km/h.

LAP RECORD:

J. Villeneuve (Williams-Renault) in 1997 :
1'18"197 at 197,089 km/h.

RACE HISTORY

1999 : M. Häkkinen (McLaren)
1998 : M. Häkkinen (Mclaren)
1997 : J. Villeneuve (Williams)
1996 : D. Hill (Williams)
1995 : M. Schumacher (Benetton)
1994 : M. Schumacher (Benetton)
1993 : A. Senna (McLaren)
1992 : N. Mansell (Williams)
1991 : A. Senna (McLaren)
1990 : A. Prost (Ferrari)
etc...

Alain Prost won the Brazilian GP six times (1982, 84, 85, 87, 88, et 90)
Emerson Fittipaldi won the first Brazil G.P. in 1973 at Interlagos.
The year 2000 will see the 28th running of the Brazilian G.P.
It took place at Interlagos from 1973 to 1978, then again in 1980, and from 1990. (18 times including 2000)
It has also been held at Jacarepagua (Rio de Janeiro) in 1978 and from 1981 to 1989. (10 times)

SAN MARINO GRAND PRIX
SUNDAY 9TH APRIL
IMOLA

1999 STATISTICS

START GRID:

1st	M. Häkkinen (McLaren-Mercedes)	1'26"362
2	D. Coulthard (McLaren-Mercedes)	1'26"384
3	M. Schumacher (Ferrari)	1'26"538
4	E. Irvine (Ferrari)	1'26"993
5	J. Villeneuve (BAR-Supertec)	1'27"313
6	R. Barrichello (Stewart-Ford)	1'27"409

etc...

RACE RESULT:

1st	M. Schumacher (Ferrari)	in 1h 33'44"792
		195,481 km/h
2	D. Coulthard (McLaren-Mercedes)	4"265
3	R. Barrichello (Stewart-Ford)	1 lap
4	D. Hill (Jordan-Mugen-Honda)	1 lap
5	G. Fisichella (Benetton-Playlife)	1 lap
6	J. Alesi (Sauber-Petronas)	1 lap
7	M. Salo (BAR-Supertec)	3 laps
8	L. Badoer (Minardi-Ford)	3 laps
9	M. Gene (Minardi-Ford)	3 laps
10	J. Herbert (Stewart-Ford)	4 laps
11	A. Zanardi (Williams-Supertec)à 4 lapss	

FASTEST LAPS 1999:

M. Schumacher (Ferrari) : 1'28"547 at 200,435 km/h

LAP RECORD:

H.-H. Frentzen (Williams-Renault) in 1997 : 1'25"531
at 207,503 km/h

RACE HISTORY

1999 : M. Schumacher (Ferrari)
1998 : D. Coulthard (McLaren)
1997 : H.-H. Frentzen (Williams)
1996 : D. Hill (Williams)
1995 : D. Hill (Williams)
1994 : M. Schumacher (Benetton)
1993 : A. Prost (Williams)
1992 : N. Mansell (Williams)
1991 : A. Senna (Mclaren)
1990 : R. Patrese (Williams)
etc...

Ayrton Senna (1988, 89 and 91) and Alain Prost (1984, 86 et 93) both won three times.

The first San Marino GP was won by Nelson Piquet (Brabham) on 3rd May 1981 at Imola.

Including this year's event there have been 20 San Marino Grands Prix.

Start : 14h00.
62 laps of 4.943 km or 306.229 km.
Attendance in 1999 : 90 000 spectators on Sunday.
Location: 35 kilometres south east of Bologna.
The nearest airports are Bologna and Forli.

The San Marino Grand Prix has traditionally marked the start of the European season. This year, despite changes to the calendar, Imola keeps its place, albeit about three weeks earlier than usual.
It is to be hoped that the last of the cool winter weather has left Italy by early April. The tifosi won't feel the cold if "la Ferrari va bene." Just as at Monza, they only have eyes for the red rockets. A good qualifying performance for the home team ensures tens of thousands of extra fans on Sunday. If the Ferraris retire during the race, a large number of spectators leave the circuit well before the chequered flag and causing never ending traffic jams. However, if Ferrari does well, then they will invade the track and hang around for hours shouting the name of their hero "Schumi" or maybe even Barrichello, while waving giant banners. It is just one of the many charms of Imola.

IMOLA AS SEEN BY JARNO TRULLI :

It is the first race in Europe and in Italy as well. The atmosphere is special. I have never had much luck at Imola. I have taken part in three grands prix here without finishing a single one. I hope I will have more luck this time. The track is very demanding with a lot of heavy braking because of the chicanes. Technically, Imola is not fantastic but we hit some high top speeds and have to brake very hard. You really feel the presence of the crowd, especially all the Ferrari fans. Of course, for all the Italian drivers, this is an important event.

Address :
Autodromo Enzo et Dino Ferrari
Via Fratelli Rosselli 2
40026 Imola (Bo) Italy
Tel : 00 39 05 42 31 444
Fax : 00 39 05 42 30 420

BRITISH GRAND PRIX
SILVERSTONE
SUNDAY 23RD APRIL 200

Start : 13h00, 14h00 in Europe.
60 laps of 5.141 km or 308.289 km.
Attendance en 1999 : 120 000 spectators on Sunday.
Location: Silverstone circuit is 110 kilometres to the north west of London, 25 kilometres to the south east of Northampton and 45 kilometres from Oxford. The nearest airports are Birmingham (50 km) London Heathrow and Luton.

"The home of motor sport" is Silverstone's motto and so it is. Most of the Formula 1 teams are based within striking distance of the former Royal Air Force airfield. This year, FIA has made some radical changes to the traditional calendar. For decades, the British Grand Prix has been held in mid-July, the best time of the year with the most chance of sunshine and the least possibility of rain.
Last year, the wet races were thrilling and full of incident. Putting on this event in April, there is a much higher chance of the race taking place in the rain. The organisers tried in vain to swop dates with Austria, but the risk of snow in Styria meant this was a non-starter. No doubt Easter weekend in the English countryside will be very interesting. Especially if you are nice and warm at home in front of the television.

SILVERSTONE AS SEEN BY JARNO TRULLI :

"I don't want to think about it. It can rain here all the time even in summer, so what will it be like in April? It is not one of my favourite races, but the atmosphere is nice. It is a very demanding track technically. It is essential to have a good understanding of the circuit and of your car. This year, driving a Jordan, built outside the circuit gates, Heinz-Harald Frentzen and I will have a slight advantage over the others."

Address :
Silverstone Circuits Ltd
Silverstone near Towcester
Northamptonshire NN 12 8TN
United Kingdom
Tel : 00 44 13 27 85 72 71
Fax : 00 44 13 27 85 76 63

1999 STATISTICS

START GRID:

1st	M. Häkkinen (McLaren-Mercedes)	1'24"804
2	M. Schumacher (Ferrari)	1'25"223
3	D. Coulthard (McLaren)	1'25"594
4	E. Irvine (Ferrari)	1'25"677
5	H.-H. Frentzen (Jordan-Mugen-Honda)	1'25"991
6	D. Hill (Jordan-Mugen-Honda)	1'26"099

RACE RESULT:

1st	D. Coulthard (McLaren-Mercedes)	in 1h32'30"144 199,970 km/h
2	E. Irvine (Ferrari)	1"829
3	R. Schumacher (Williams-Renault)	27"411
4	H.-H. Frentzen (Jordan-Mugen-Honda)	27"789
5	D. Hill (Jordan-Mugen-Honda)	38"606
6	P. Diniz (Sauber-Petronas)	53"643
7	G. Fisichella (Benetton-Playlife)	54"614
8	R. Barrichello (Stewart-Ford)	1'8"590
9	J. Trulli (Peugeot-Prost)	1'12"045
10	A. Wurz (Benetton-Playlife)	1'15"123
11	A. Zanardi (Williams-Supertec)	1'17"124
12	J. Herbert (Stewart-Ford)	1'17"709
13	O. Panis (Prost-Peugeot)	1'20"492
14	J. Alesi (Sauber-Petronas)	1 lap
15	M. Gene (Minardi-Ford)	2 laps
16	T. Takagi (Arrows)	2 laps

FASTEST LAPS 1999:
M. Häkkinen (McLaren-Mercedes) : 1'28"309 at 209.536 km/h

LAP RECORD:
M. Schumacher (Ferrari) in 1997 : 1'24"475 at 219.047 km/h

RACE HISTORY

1999 : D. Coulthard (McLaren)
1998 : M. Schumacher (Ferrari)
1997 : J. Villeneuve (Williams)
1996 : J. Villeneuve (Williams)
1995 : J. Herbert (Benetton)
1994 : D. Hill (Williams)
1993 : A. Prost (Williams)
1992 : N. Mansell (Williams)
1991 : N. Mansell (Williams)
1990 : A. Prost (Ferrari)

Alain Prost (1983, 85, 89, 90 et 93) and Jim Clark (1962, 63, 64, 65 et 67) each won this event five times.
Nino Farinawon the first British Grand Prix on 1st May 1950 at the wheel of an Alfa Rom≠o at Silverstone.
The 2000 race will be the 51st edition of the British Grand Prix.
It has been run 34 times at Silverstone (from 1950 to 58, in 60, 63, 65, 67, 69, 71, 73, 75, 77, 79, 81, 83, 85, and from 87 to 2000).
Il has been held at Brands Hatch twelve times (1964, 66, 68, 70, 72, 74, 76, 78, 80, 82, 84 and 86) it also took place at Aintree five times, 1955, 57, 59, 61 et 62.

SPANISH GRAND PRIX
SUNDAY 7TH MAY 2000
BARCELONA

1999 STATISTICS

START GRID:

1st	M. Häkkinen (McLaren-Mercedes)	1'22"088
2	E. Irvine (Ferrari)	1'22"219
3	D. Coulthard (McLaren-Mercedes)	1'22"244
4	M. Schumacher (Ferrari)	1'22"277
5	J. Alesi (Sauber-Petronas)	1'22"388
6	J. Villeneuve (Bar-Supertec)	1'22"703

etc...

RACE RESULT:

1st	M. Häkkinen (McLaren-Mercedes)	in 1h34'13"665
		195,608km/h
2	D. Coulthard (McLaren-Mercedes)	6"238
3	M. Schumacher (Ferrari)	10"845
4	E. Irvine (Ferrari)	30"182
5	R. Schumacher (Williams-Supertec)	1'27"208
6	J. Trulli (Prost-Peugeot)	1 lap
7	D. Hill (Jordan-Mugen-Honda)	1 lap
8	M. Salo (BAR-Supertec)	1 lap
9	G. Fisichella (Benetton-Playlife)	1 lap
10	A. Wurz (Benetton-Playlife)	1 laps
11	P. De la Rosa (Arrows)	2 laps
12	T. Takagi (Arrows)	3 laps

FASTEST LAPS 1999:

M. Schumacher (Ferrari) : 1'24"982 at 200,287 km/h

LAP RECORD:

G. Fisichella (Jordan-Peugeot) in 1997 : 1'22"242 at 206,960 km/h.

RACE HISTORY

1999 : M. Häkkinen (McLaren)
1998 : M. Häkkinen (McLaren)
1997 : J. Villeneuve (Williams)
1996 : M. Schumacher (Ferrari)
1995 : M. Schumacher (Benetton)
1994 : D. Hill (Williams)
1993 : A. Prost (Williams)
1992 : N. Mansell (Williams)
1991 : N. Mansell (Williams)
1990 : A. Prost (Ferrari)
etc...
Alain Prost (1988, 90 and 93) and Jackie Stewart (1969, 70 and 73) won the Spanish GP three times.

Juan Manuel Fangio won the first Spanish Grand Prix at Pedralbles on 28th October 1951 in an Alfa Romeo.

2000 will mark the thirtieth running of the Spanish Grand Prix.
- Twice at Pedralbles (Barcelona) 1951 and 54
- 9 times at Jarama (Madrid) 1968, 70, 72, 74, 76, 77, 78, 79 et 81
- 4 times at Montjuich (Barcelona) 1969, 71, 73 et 75
- 5 times at Jerez 1986, 87, 88, 89 et 90
- 10 times at Catalunya (Barcelona) 1991 to 2000

Start: 14h00.
65 laps of 4.766 km or 309.663 km
Attendance in 1999 : 81 000 spectators on Sunday.
Location: The circuit is 20 kilometres to the north east of Barcelona. The nearest airports are Barcelona to the south and Gerona in the north. The motorway from France to Barcelona passes within one kilometre of the circuit.

The presence of two Spanish drivers and national sponsors in the closed world of Formula 1 drivers goes a long way towards explaining the renewed interest in the sport in this part of the world. Since last year, the grandstands at the Catalunya circuit have started to fill up, although it is not quite a sell-out in the style of the Nou Camp soccer stadium in Barcelona.
It is an ultra modern circuit, built at the same time as the 1992 Olympic Games and it fits in perfectly with the draconian rules of F1 in the year 2000. Vast pits, a wide track and wider run-off areas at the danger points and a track that twists and turns so that spectators can see most of the action, along with easy access, means that this track is from the same breed as Magny Cours or Sepang. Mild winters and a technically challenging track make it a favourite testing venue for most teams. Sadly, the Montmelo circuit lacks character or charm and is situated in the middle of nowhere.

BARCELONA AS SEEN BY JARNO TRULLI :

"It's a nice circuit and I enjoy driving here in Barcelona. I have a lot of experience at this track now. Last year, I scored a point after a difficult race. It is a very demanding track technically, which is why we all do a lot of testing here as we get a lot of feed back to help set up the car. There is not much reaction from the fans, as the crowd is so small, but the city of Barcelona is an added attraction."

Address :
Circuit de Catalunya
Carretera de Granollers, km 2
08160 Montmelo (Ba) Spain
Tel : 00 34 35 71 97 00
Fax : 00 34 35 71 30 61

EUROPEAN GRAND PRIX
NURBURGRING

SUNDAY 21ST MAY 2000

Start : 14h00.
67 laps of 4.567 km or 305.989 km.
1999 Attendance : 130 000 spectators on Sunday.
Location: The Nurbrugring is 90 kilometres to the south west of Cologne and 60 kilometres north west of Koblenz. The main airports are Cologne and Dusseldorf (120 km.) The area is cris-crossed with several motorways, but getting out of the circuit on Sunday night is a nightmare!

For ever in the shadow of the mysterious Nurburg castle, this circuit will enter the new millenium hosting Formula 1 for the twenty ninth time. At first it staged the German Grand Prix, until Niki Lauda's terrible accident in 1976. At the time the track was 22.835 kilometres in length and only fourteen laps were required to make up a race distance. For just a few marks you can drive round this old track yourself. It is certainly worth making a detour for this ride of a lifetime. Having been banished from the Formula 1 calendar, a new 'Ring was built on the southern part to give us the circuit we know today.
It has an immense stadium with giant television screens for the spectators. Sadly, this area often falls victim to the capricious weather gods, but it does not stop the German fans turning out in their droves.

THE NURBURGRING AS SEEN BY JARNO TRULLI :

"This is one of my favourite circuits, apart from the cold weather. I am happy to go to the Nurburgring, even though I hate the cold. I know the track well and I soon get into a rhythm. I did some very quick laps in my Formula 3 days and last year I scored my first ever F1 podium here. It makes me want to go back as it seems to be a lucky circuit for me."

Address :
N(tm)rburgring Gmbh
5489 N(tm)rburg/ Eifel
Germany
Tel : 00 49 26 01 30 20
Fax : 00 49 26 91 302 155

1999 STATISTICS

START GRID:

1st	H.-H. Frentzen (Jordan-Mugen-Honda)	1'19"910
2	D. Coulthard (McLaren-Mercedes)	1'20"176
3	M. Häkkinen (McLaren-Mercedes)	1'20"376
4	R. Schumacher (Williams-Supertec)	1'20"444
5	O. Panis (Prost-Peugeot)	1'20"638
6	G. Fisichella (Benetton-Playlife)	1'20"781

etc...

RACE RESULT:

1st	H.-H. Herbert (Stewart-Ford)	in 1h41'54"314
		177,034 km/h
2	J. Trulli (Prost-Peugeot)	22"618
3	R. Barrichello (Stewart-Ford)	22"865
4	R. Schumacher (Williams-Supertec)	39"507
5	M. Häkkinen (McLaren-Mercedes)	1'02"950
6	M. Gene (Minardi-Ford)	1'05"154
7	E. Irvine (Ferrari)	1'06"683
8	R. Zonta (BAR-Supertec)	1 lap
9	O. Panis (Prost-Peugeot)	1 lap
10	J. Villeneuve (BAR-Supertec)	5 laps

FASTEST LAPS 1999:

M. Häkkinen (McLaren-Mercedes) : 1'21"282 at 201,786 km/h

LAP RECORD:

H.-H. Frentzen (Williams-Renault) in 1997 : 1'18"805 at 208,128 km/h.

RACE HISTORY

Since the new Nurburgring was built, there have only been six grands prix held here.

1999 : J. Herbert (Stewart)
1998 : M. Häkkinen (McLaren)
1997 : J. Villeneuve (Williams)
1996 : J. Villeneuve (Williams)
1995 : M. Schumacher (Benetton)
1984 : A. Prost (McLaren)

2000 will mark the tenth European Grand Prix.

- twice at Brands Hatch (1983 and 85)
- 4 times at the N(tm)rburgring (1984, 95 , 96, 99 and 2000)
- once at Donington (1993)
- twice at Jerez (1994 et 97)

MONACO GRAND PRIX
SUNDAY 4TH JUNE 2000
MONTE CARLO

1999 STATISTICS

START GRID:

1st	M. Häkkinen (McLaren-Mercedes)	1'20"547
2	M. Schumacher (Ferrari)	1'20"611
3	D. Coulthard (McLaren-Mercedes)	1'20"956
4	E. Irvine (Ferrari)	1'21"011
5	R. Barrichello (Stewart-Ford)	1'21"530
6	H.-H. Frentzen (Jordan-Mugen-Honda)	1'21"656

etc...

RACE RESULT:

1st	M. Schumacher (Ferrari)	in 1h49"31"812
		143,864 km/h
2	E. Irvine (Ferrari)	30"476
3	M. Häkkinen (Mclaren-Mercedes)	37"483
4	H.-H. Frentzen (Jordan-Mugen-Honda)	54"009
5	G. Fisichella (Benetton-Playlife)	1 la
6	A. Wurz (Benetton-Playlife)	1 lap
7	J. Trulli (Prost-Peugeot)	1 lap
8	A. Zanardi (Williams-Supertec)	2 laps
9	R. Barrichello (Stewart-Ford)	7 laps

LAP RECORD:

M. Häkkinen (McLaren-Mercedes) : 1'22"259 at 147,354 km/h.

RACE HISTORY

1999 : M. Schumacher (Ferrari)
1998 : M. Häkkinen (McLaren)
1997 : M. Schumacher (Ferrari)
1996 : O. Panis (Ligier)
1995 : M. Schumacher (Benetton)
1994 : M.Schumacher (Benetton)
1993 : A. Senna (McLaren)
1992 : A. Senna (McLaren)
1991 : A. Senna (McLaren)
1990 : A. Senna (McLaren)
etc...

Ayrton Senna holds the record for wins in Monaco with six to his name (1987, 89, 90, 91, 92 and 93).
Graham Hill won five times (1963, 64, 65, 68 and 69)
Alain Prost triumphed on four occasions (1984, 85, 86 and 88)
Juan Manuel Fangio won the first Monaco Grand Prix, which counted for the world championship on 21st May 1950 in an Alfa Romeo.

Start : 14h00.
78 laps of 3378 km or 263.484 km.
Attendance in 1999 : 120 000 spectators on Sunday.
Location: the circuit is situated 18 kilometres to the east of Nice and is run in the streets of the Principality of Monaco. The nearest airport is at Nice. Monte Carlo can then be reached by road, train or helicopter.

Traditionally, the Monaco Grand Prix is held on the weekend of Ascension, a religious festival with a changeable date, which this years falls at the beginning of June.
Without doubt, it is the most prestigious event on the calendar and it is the most famous in the world. That is understandable as no other race offers as much charm and glamour. The actual racing through the streets is an impressive spectacle and the noise from the engines is deafening. It has it all, what with good organisation, a host of stars who drop in from the Cannes Film Festival, a bevy of goddesses and the Mediterranean as a back drop. In short, the Monaco fairy tale has it all.
However, there are some who say it is an anachronism, unsuited to modern F1 cars, that it is riddled with snobbery, the police are draconian, the traffic is a nightmare. But if you can afford it, do not hesitate to make the trip for this weekend in Monte Carlo. If you only ever see one grand prix in your life you must make it the Monaco Grand Prix, as long as you do it properly and have a good grandstand seat from which to lap up the action.

MONACO AS SEEN BY JARNO TRULLI :

"This is my home race, as I live in Monte Carlo. The track is very difficult and extremely demanding physically. It is different in that it is not a permanent track and you just have to try and set up the car as best you can.
I have always gone well in Monaco and I have always had a good race. Unfortunately, I have never managed to finish and my luck has always run out. I hope that changes this year and that I get a good result as well. Monaco is different to all the other grands prix, because of its unique and colourful atmosphere."

Address :
Automobile Club de Monaco
23, Bd Albert 1er
BP 464, 98012 Monaco Cedex
Tel : 00 377 93 15 26 00
Fax : 00 377 93 25 80 08

CANADIAN GRAND PRIX
MONTREAL

SUNDAY 18TH JUNE 2000

Start : 13h00 local time, 19h00 in Europe.
69 laps of 4.427 km or 305463 km
Attendance : 73 000 spectators.
Location : The circuit is just a few kilometres from the centre of Montreal on the Ile Notre Dame, former site of the World Fair and some events of the 1976 Olympic Games.

No need to take the car as the Metro take you right to the track. Jacques Villeneuve has been responsible for boosting spectator figures. For the past two years, the first corner has provided more than its fair share of excitement with plenty of accidents, thankfully free of injury.
It is a popular event because of the warm welcome provided by the people of Quebec, the proximity to the United States and the fact it is only a six hour flight from Europe.

MONTREAL SEEN BY JARNO TRULLI :

"I quite like Montreal; the city, the people and life in Canada. I am happy to come here where the fans are very enthusiastic. It is a nice grand prix. I have confidence in the track, despite coming to grief at the first corner for the past two years. This year, that won't happen, as I will start from the front."

Address :
Circuit Gilles Villeneuve
Bassin Olympique
Ile Notre Dame
Montréal, Québec H3C 1A0
Canada.
Tel : 00 1 514 350 47 31
Fax : 00 1 514 350 00 07

1999 STATISTICS

START GRID:

1st	M. Schumacher (Ferrari)	1'19"298
2	M. Häkkinen (McLaren-Mercedes)	1'19"237
3	E. Irvine (Ferrari)	1'19"440
4	D. Coulthard (McLaren-Mercedes)	1'19"729
5	R. Barrichello (Stewart-Ford)	1'19"930
6	H.-H. Frentzen (Jordan-Mugen-Honda)	1'20"158

etc...

RACE RESULT:

1st	M. Häkkinen (McLaren-Mercedes)	in 1h41'35"727
		180,155 km/h
2	G. Fisichella (Benetton-Playlife)	0"781
3	E. Irvine (Ferrari)	1"796
4	R. Schumacher (Williams-Supertec)	2"391
5	J. Herbert (Stewart-Ford)	2"804
6	P. Diniz (Sauber-Petronas)	3"710
7	D. Coulthard (McLaren-Mercedes)	5"003
8	M. Gene (Minardi-Ford)	1 lap
9	O. Panis (Prost-Peugeot)	1 lap
10	L. Badoer (Minardi-Ford)	2 laps
11	H.-H. Frentzen (Jordan-Mugen-Honda)	4 laps

FASTEST LAPS 1999:
Eddie Irvine (Ferrari) : 1'20"382 at 197,999 km/h.
LAP RECORD:
Michael Schumacher (Ferrari) en 1998 : 1'19"379 at 200,501 km/h.

RACE HISTORY

1999 : M. Häkkinen (McLaren)
1998 : M. Schumacher (Ferrari)
1997 : M. Schumacher (Ferrari)
1996 : D. Hill (Williams)
1995 : J. Alesi (Ferrari)
1994 : M. Schumacher (Benetton)
1993 : A. Prost (Williams)
1992 : G. Berger (McLaren)
1991 : N. Piquet (Benetton)
1990 : A. Senna (McLaren)
etc...

Nelson Piquet won three times in Canada in 1982, 84 and 91 as did Michael Schumacher in 1994, 97 and 98.
The first Canadian Grand Prix was won by Jack Brabham
on 27th August 1967 in a Brabham-Repco at Mosport.
2000 will mark the 32nd running of the Canadian Grand Prix.
It was run eight times atMosport (1967, 69, 71, 72, 73, 74, 76 and 77), twice at Mont Tremblant (1968 and 70) et twenty two times at Montréal (from 1978 to 1986 and since 1988).

1999 STATISTICS

START GRID:

1st	R. Barrichello (Stewart-Ford)	1'38"441
2	J. Alesi (Sauber-Petronas)	1'38"881
3	O. Panis (Prost-Peugeot)	1'40"400
4	D. Coulthard (McLaren-Mercedes)	1'40"403
5	H.-H. Frentzen (Jordan-Mugen-Honda)	1'40"690
6	M. Schumacher (Ferrari)	1'41"127

etc...

RACE RESULT:

1st	H.-H. Frentzen (Jordan-Mugen-Honda) in 1h 58'24"343	
		154,965 km/h
2	M. Häkkinen (McLaren-Mercedes)	11"092
3	R. Barrichello (Stewart-Ford)	43"432
4	R. Schumacher (Williams-Supertec)	45"475
5	M. Schumacher (Ferrari)	47"881
6	E. Irvine (Ferrari)	48"901
7	J. Trulli (Prost-Peugeot)	57"771
8	O. Panis (Prost-Peugeot)	58"531
9	R. Zonta (BAR-Supertec)	1'28"764
10	L. Badoer (Minardi-Ford)	1 lap
11	T. Takagi (Arrows)	1 lap
12	P. De la Rosa (Arrows)	1 lap

FASTEST LAPS 1999:

D. Coulthard (McLaren-Mercedes) : 1'19"227 at 193,115 km/h

LAP RECORD:

N. Mansell (Williams-Renault) in 1992 : 1'17"070 at 198,521 km/h.

RACE HISTORY

1999 : H.-H.. Frentzen (Jordan)
1998 : M. Schumacher (Ferrari)
1997 : M. Schumacher (Ferrari)
1996 : D. Hill (Williams)
1995 : M. Schumacher (Benetton)
1994 : M. Schumacher (Benetton)
1993 : A. Prost (Williams)
1992 : N. Mansell (Williams)
1991 : N. Mansell (Williams)
1990 : A. Prost (Ferrari)
etc...

Schumacher did it on four occasions (1994, 95, 97 and 98).
Juan Manuel Fangio won the first French GP at Reims on 2nd July 1950 at the wheel of an Alfa Romeo.

2000 will be the fiftieth running of the French Grand Prix.
- Reims :1950, 51, 53, 54, 56, 58, 59, 60, 61, 63 and 66. (11 times)
- Rouen :1952, 57, 62, 64 and 68. (5 times)
- Clermont-Ferrand :1965, 69, 70 and 72. (4 times)
- Le Mans : 1967.
- Le Castellet : 1971, 73, 75, 76, 78, 80, 82, 83, 85, 86, 87, 88, 89 and 90. (14 times)
- Dijon-Prenois :1974, 77, 79, 81 and 84. (5 times)
- Magny-Cours : from 1991 to 2000. (10 times)

Start : 14h00.
72 laps of 4248 km or 305.670 km.
Attendance : 106 000 spectators on Sunday.
Location: The Nevers circuit is 12 kilometres south of Nevers, 250 km south of Paris and 220 km north of Lyon. The area is not well served by motorways and so getting there and especially getting home again, requires a degree of patience.

When Bernie Ecclestone bought the Paul Ricard circuit last May, doubts were cast over the future of the French GP in the Nievre region. However, in the short term at least, Magny Cours seems to have secured its future.
Any popularity charts of Formula 1 venues inevitably pick Magny Cours as the least popular venue of the year. It has hosted the French Grand Prix since 1991. With Switzerland and Germany not too far away, the race always gets a good crowd. As an ultra-modern track it is, along with Barcelona, one of the safest tracks in the world.
The only real cloud on the horizon is the feeble number of hotel beds in the area. The locals have used this fact to charge exorbitant amounts for simple bed and breakfast accommodation, which would cost just a fraction as much in England or Germany. However, occasionally one can find charming little out of the way spots where the food is excellent.

MAGNY COURS AS SEEN BY JARNO TRULLI :

"This is a second homecoming for me. Magny Cours holds all sorts of memories for me as it is where I drove the Prost for the very first time. I have a good feeling for this track and have had some good races here. I will be reunited with fans who gave me a lot of support when I was with Prost, but I suppose they will have changed allegiance this time! Nevertheless, I am looking forward to coming to France."

Address :
Circuit de Magny-Cours
Technopole
58470 Magny-Cours, France.
Tél : 03 86 21 00 00
Fax : 03 86 21 80 80

AUSTRIAN GRAND PRIX
SPIELBERG
SUNDAY 16TH JULY 2000

Start : 14h00.
71 laps of 4.338 km or 307.998 km.
Attendance in 1999 : 60 000 spectators on Sunday.
Location: Situated right in the middle of the country, the A1 Ring, formerly the Osterreichring is 200 kilometres from the major Austrian cities; 200 km south west of Vienna and a hundred to the north west of Graz. The motorway passes within a kilometre of the circuit entrance. Watch out for radar traps and massive traffic jams heading back for Vienna on Sunday night!

This grand prix is run against the most spectacular backdrop of the year, with the pine forests, the mountains and the Tyrolean atmosphere. The locals offer a warm welcome and the track is like a toboggan run. All in all, Zeltweg is a great place for a race. The one cloud on the horizon is literally that. Violent storms can hit the area on a regular basis at the end of the afternoon, flooding the camp sites. The campers drown their sorrows with copious amounts of beer, while those staying in the little gasthofs can appreciate the dry.
The Austrian GP had been off the calendar for ten years until 1997. The old Osterreichring was one of the fastest tracks in the world with its daunting "Bosch Curve" which none but the brave took flat out. The new track is a shadow of its former self, but it is still very much worth a visit. Come and see for yourself!

SPIELBERG AS SEEN BY JARNO TRULLI :
"Along with France, this is an other track that holds pleasant memories for me. In 1997, I was lucky enough to lead the race for several laps. It is a beautiful circuit which is not very demanding, but you need to settle into a rhythm and find the right lines to be quick. The atmosphere at this grand prix is great and a lot of Italian fans make the journey which is nice for me."

Address :
A1- Ring
A 8724 Spielberg/Stmk
Austria
Tel : 00 43 35 77 753
Fax : 00 43 35 77 753 107

1999 STATISTICS

START GRID:

1st	M. Häkkinen (McLaren-Mercedes)	1'10"954
2	D. Coulthard (McLaren-Mercedes)	1'11"153
3	E. Irvine (Ferrari)	1'11"973
4	H.-H. Frentzen (Jordan-Mugen-Honda)	1'12"266
5	R. Barrichello (Stewart-Ford)	1'12"342
6	J. Herbert (Stewart-Ford)	1'12"488

etc...

RACE RESULT:

1st	E. Irvine (Ferrari)	in 1h28'12"438 208,587 km/h
2	D. Coulthard (McLaren-Mercedes)	0"313
3	M. Häkkinen (McLaren-Mercedes)	22"282
4	H.-H. Frentzen (Jordan-Mugen-Honda)	52"803
5	A.Wurz (Benetton-Playlife)	1'6"358
6	P. Diniz (Sauber)	1'10"933
7	J. Trulli (Prost-Peugeot)	1 lap
8	D. Hill (Jordan-Mugen-Honda)	1 lap
9	M. Salo (Ferrari)	1 lap
10	O. Panis (Prost-Peugeot)	1 lap
11	M. Gene (Minardi-Ford)	1 lap
12	G. Fisichella (Benetton-Playlife)	3 laps
13	L. Badoer (Minardi-Ford)	3 laps
14	J. Herbert (Stewart-Ford)	4 laps
15	R. Zonta (BAR-Supertec)	8 laps

FASTEST LAPS 1999:

M. Häkkinen (McLaren-Mercedes) ein 1'12"107 at 215,629 km/h

RACE HISTORY

1999 : E. Irvine (Ferrari)
1998 : M. Häkkinen (McLaren)
1997 : J. Villeneuve (Williams)
1987 : N. Mansell (Williams)
1986 : A. Prost (McLaren)
1985 : A. Prost (McLaren)
1984 : N. Lauda (McLaren)
1983 : A. Prost (Renault)
1982 : E. de Angelis (Lotus)
1981 : J. Laffite (Ligier)
1980 : J.P. Jabouille (Renault)
etc...

Alain Prost won three Austrian GP (1983, 85 and 86)
Lorenzo Bandini won the first Austrian Grand Prix on 23rd August 1964 in a Ferrari.
2000 will see the 23rd Austrian Grand Prix. Run at Zeltweg, ever since 1964 when it was held at the airfield, it became the ´sterreichring from 1970 to 1987, then A1-Ring since 1997.

GERMAN GRAND PRIX
SUNDAY 30TH JULY 2000
HOCKEINHEIM

1999 STATISTICS

START GRID:

1st	M. Häkkinen (McLaren-Mercedes)	1'42"950
2	H.-H. Frentzen (Jordan-Mugen-Honda)	1'43"000
3	D. Coulthard (McLaren-Mercedes)	1'43"288
4	M. Salo (Ferrari)	1'43"577
5	E. Irvine (Ferrari)	1'43"769
6	R. Barrichello (Stewart-Ford)	1'43"938

etc...

RACE RESULT:

1st	E. Irvine (Ferrari)	in 1h21'58"594
		224,723 km/h
2	M. Salo (Ferrari)	1"007
3	H.-H. Frentzen (Jordan-Mugen-Honda)	5"195
4	R. Schumacher (Williams-Supertec)	12"809
5	D. Coulthard (McLaren-Mercedes)	16"823
6	O. Panis (Prost-Peugeot)	29"819
7	A. Wurz (Benetton-Playlife)	33"333
8	J. Alesi (Sauber-Petronas)	1'11"291
9	M. Gene (Minardi-Ford)	1'48"318
10	L. Badoer (Minardi-Ford)	1 lap
11	J. Herbert (Stewart-Ford)	5 laps

LAP RECORD:

D. Coulthard (McLaren-Mercedes) in 1'45"270
at 233,331 km/h.

RACE HISTORY

1999 : E. Irvine (Ferrari)
1998 : M. Häkkinen (McLaren)
1997 : G. Berger (Benetton)
1996 : D. Hill (Williams)
1995 : M. Schumacher (Benetton)
1994 : G. Berger (Ferrari)
1993 : A. Prost (Williams)
1992 : N. Mansell (Williams)
1991 : N. Mansell (Williams)
1990 : A. Senna (McLaren)
etc...

Juan Manuel Fangio (1954, 56 and 57), Nelson Piquet
(1981, 86 and 87) and Ayrton Senna (1988, 89 and 90)
all won three times in Germany.
Alberto Ascari (Alfa Romeo) won the first German Grand
Prix on 29th July 1951 at the N(tm)rburgring.
2000 will be the 48th running of the German Grand Prix.
The national G.P. took place 23 times at the N(tm)rbur-
gring
(from 1951 to 1954, from 1956 to 1958, from 1961 to
69, from 71 to 76 and since 1985).
It was held just once at Avus in Berlin in 1959.
Finally, it has been held 24 times at Hockenheim in
1970, from 1977 to 84, and since 1986.

Start : 14h00.
46 laps of 6.749 km, or 310.454 km.
Attendance in 1999: 102 000 spectators on Sunday.
Location: The circuit is 90 kilometres to the south of Frankfurt, 110 to the north east
of Stuttgart and around twenty from the magnificent city of Heidelberg. Surrounded by
motorways, it is easily accessible. However, do not wait to long to leave after the race.
As the camp sites empty, the inevitable traffic jams begin.

After Jim Clark was killed here in 1967 during an F2 race on this very fast track, two chicanes were built on the long straights to slow the cars down. In order to further lower the
average speed, a third chicane was added at a later date. Today there is talk of reducing
the track length as the long run through the forest is of little interest.
Last year, the absence of Michael Schumacher after his Silverstone accident, dampened the
ardour of the German fans. The camp sites filled up all the same and were their usual pic-
turesque sight. This year we can expect to see a return to the good old days with Schumi's
army of fans in fine voice again. On top of that, they will have Schumi-junior, Frentzen and
Heidfeld to cheer as well.

HOCKENHEIM AS SEEN BY JARNO TRULLI :

"This is one of my favourite tracks. In 1996 in F3, I won
all six of the races run at Hockenheim, taking pole position and lap record every time! I have always had a better understanding of this track than my rivals and
managed to make the most of that. In 1997, I even
managed to come fourth in the Prost. The circuit looks
easy because of the long straights, but that is wrong.
There are some heavy braking points and the stadium
section is difficult. It is quite a demanding track and the
crowd is also very impressive."

Address :
Hockeinheimring
Gmbh Motodrom,
Postfach 1106
68754 Hockeinheim
Germany
Tel : 00 49 62 05 95 00
Fax : 00 49 62 05 95 02 10

HUNGARIAN GRAND PRIX
BUDAPEST
SUNDAY 13TH AUGUST 2000

Start : 14h00.
77 laps of 3.976 km, or 306.152 km.
Attendance in 1999 : 95 000 spectators on Sunday.
Location: The Hungaroring is 20 kilometres to the north east of Budapest and Ferihegy, its international airport. The M3 motorway leads to the circuit. To make a quick getaway on Sunday night, slip into one of the many police-escorted convoys traveling to the airport. Budapest is certainly worth a visit - one of the most beautiful cities in Europe and full of history.

Back in 1986, Trabants roamed the streets, young girls stood at the side of the road offering local accommodation and the grandstands were packed. Much has changed since the collapse of the Iron Curtain and Hungary has transformed itself in the space of ten years. The cost of tickets has unfortunately spiraled and so the average Hungarian cannot afford to attend his home grand prix. A grandstand seat costs the equivalent of several months's salary. So it is left to the Germans, the Austrians and now the Finns to make the journey and fill the enclosures.
The grandstands in Budapest are some of the most colourful and noisy of the year. The weather is usually excellent and the weekend has a party atmosphere. It is the ideal venue to combine a grand prix and a holiday, as long as you can put up with the gypsy violinists to be found in every restaurant.

BUDAPEST AS SEEN BY JARNO TRULLI :

"It is a nice circuit which I look forward to. The fact it is always hot, that there are lots of corners and it is a long race, make it a very tiring event. It seems designed with the sole purpose of exhausting the drivers. You have to be fit when you get there."

Address :
Hungaroring
2146 Mogyorod PO Box 10
Hungary
Tel : 00 36 28 44 44 44
Fax : 00 36 28 44 18 60

1999 STATISTICS

START GRID:

1st	M. Häkkinen (McLaren-Mercedes)	1'18"156
2	E. Irvine (Ferrari)	1'18"263
3	D. Coulthard (McLaren-Mercedes)	1'18"384
4	G. Fisichella (Benetton-Playlife)	1'18"515
5	H.-H. Frentzen (Jordan-Mugen-Honda)	1'18"664
6	D. Hill (Jordan-Mugen-Honda)	1'18"667

etc...

RACE RESULT:

1st	M. Häkkinen (McLaren-Mercedes)	in 1h46'23"536 172,524km/h
2	D. Coulthard (McLaren-Mercedes)	9'706
3	E. Irvine (Ferrari)	27"228
4	H.-H. Frentzen (Jordan-Mugen-Honda)	31"815
5	R. Barrichello (Stewart-Ford)	43"808
6	D. Hill (Jordan-Mugen-Honda)	55"726
7	A. Wurz (Benetton-Playlife)	1'1"012
8	J. Trulli (Prost-Peugeot)	1 lap
9	R. Schumacher (Williams-Supertec)	1 lap
10	O. Panis (Prost-Peugeot)	1 lap
11	J. Herbert (Stewart-Ford)	1 lap
12	M. Salo (Ferrari)	2 laps
13	R. Zonta (BAR-Supertec)	2 laps
14	L. Badoer (Minardi-Ford)	2 laps
15	P. de la Rosa (Arrows)	2 laps
16	J. Alesi (Sauber-Petronas)	3 laps
17	M. Gene (Minardi-Ford)	3 laps

FASTEST LAPS 1999:

D. Coulthard (McLaren-Mercedes) in 1'20"699 at 177,191 km/h.

LAP RECORD:

H.-H. Frentzen (Williams-Renault) en 1997 in 1'18"372 at 182,269 km/h.

RACE HISTORY

1999 : M. Häkkinen (McLaren)
1998 : M. Schumacher (Ferrari)
1997 : J. Villeneuve (Williams)
1996 : J. Villeneuve (Williams)
1995 : D. Hill (Williams)
1994 : M. Schumacher (Benetton)
1993 : D. Hill (Williams)
1992 : A. Senna (McLaren)
1991 : A. Senna (McLaren)
1990 : T. Boutsen (Williams)

Ayrton Senna was a three times winner in Budapest, in 1988, 91 and 92.
Nelson Piquet won the first Hungarian Grand Prix in a Williams on 10th August 1986.

2000 will see the 15th running of the Hungarian Grand Prix, which has always been run at the Hongaroring.

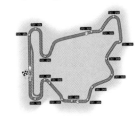

BELGIAN GRAND PRIX

SUNDAY 27TH AUGUST 2000

SPA-FRANCORCHAMPS

1999 STATISTICS

START GRID:

1st	M. Häkkinen (McLaren-Mercedes)	1'50"329
2	D. Coulthard (McLaren-Mercedes)	1'50"484
3	H.-H.. Frentzen (Jordan-Mugen-Honda)	1'51"332
4	D. Hill (Jordan-Mugen-Honda)	1'51"372
5	R. Schumacher (Williams-Supertec)	1'51"414
6	E. Irvine (Ferrari)	1'51"895

etc...

RACE RESULT:

1st	D. Coulthard (McLaren-Mercedes)	in 1h25'43"057
		214,595 km/h
2	M. Häkkinen (McLaren-Mercedes)	10"469
3	H.-H. Frentzen (Jordan-Mugen-Honda)	33"433
4	E. Irvine (Ferrari)	44"948
5	R. Schumacher (Williams-Supertec)	48"067
6	D. Hill (Jordan-Mugen-Honda)	54"916
7	M. Salo (Ferrari)	56"249
8	A. Zanardi (Williams-Supertec)	1'07"022
9	J. Alesi (Sauber-Petronas)	1'13"848
10	R. Barrichello (Stewart-Ford)	1'20"742
11	G. Fisichella (Benetton-Playlife)	1'32"195
12	J. Trulli (Prost-Peugeot)	1'36"154
13	O. Panis (Prost-Peugeot)	1'41"543
14	A. Wurz (Benetton-Playlife)	1'57"745
15	J. Villeneuve (BAR-Supertec)	1 lap
16	M. Gene (Minardi-Ford)	1 lap

FASTEST LAPS 1999:

M. Häkkinen (McLaren-Mercedes) in 1'53"955
at 220,128 km/h.

LAP RECORD:

J. Villeneuve (Williams-Renault) en 1997 in 1'52"692 at
22,596 km/h.

RACE HISTORY

1999 :	D. Coulthard (McLaren)
1998 :	D. Hill (Jordan)
1997 :	M. Schumacher (Ferrari)
1996 :	M. Schumacher (Ferrari)
1995 :	M. Schumacher (Benetton)
1994 :	D. Hill (Williams)
1993 :	D. Hill (Williams)
1992 :	M. Schumacher (Benetton)
1991 :	A. Senna (McLaren)
1990 :	A. Senna (McLaren)

etc...

Ayrton Senna won five times at Spa (1985, 88, 89, 90 and 91)
Jim Clark scored four wins (1962, 63, 64 and 65) as has Michael
Schumacher (1992, 95, 96 and 97).
Juan Manuel Fangio won the first Belgian Grand Prix at the
wheel of an Alfa Romeo on 18th June 1950 at Spa -
Francorchamps.
2000 will see the 47th running of the Belgian Grand Prix.
It has been run 35 times at Spa-Francorchamps, from 1950 to 56,
in 58, from 60 to 68, in 70, 83 and from 1985.
It was held twice at Nivelles (1972 and 74).
It was also held 10 times at Zolder (1973, 75, 76, 77, 78, 79, 80,
81, 82 and 84).

Start : 14h00.
44 laps of 6.967 km or 306.548 km.
Attendance : 86 000 spectators on Sunday.
Location: The Spa-Francorchamps circuit is situated in the east of Belgium in the
Walloon region, halfway between Luxembourg and Brussels. It is 50 kilometres south east
of Liege and the same distance from Aix-la-Chapelle and a hundred from Brussels.

After a close call with anti-tobacco legislation after wrangles between the national and local
government which banned advertising at the last Belgian Grand Prix, the event nearly disappeared from the calendar. Every driver's favourite track nearly went out the window, but in the
end reason prevailed.

The circuit is one of the last links with motor sport's past and thanks to the fact it is close to
Germany, it will always be popular as thousands of fans pour across the border to see Michael
Schumacher in action on his favourite track. The rain is a permanent feature in the Ardennes,
with hardly a single race weekend going by without at least one downpour. When the sun
shines it is a fabulous place. A sudden storm triggered the biggest crash in the history of the
sport which accounted for thirteen cars at the start of the 1998 race.

If you still want to go, make sure you take warm and waterproof clothing. Even though the
Belgian Grand Prix takes place on the final weekend in August, the temperatures can plummet
to somewhere between three and four degrees first thing in the morning!

SPA AS SEEN BY JARNO TRULLI :

"This is one of my favourite tracks. Actually, it is the one
where I have the most fun. I have happy memories of
Spa. However, I don't like the weather. Too often, the
rain messes up the results. If it was always run in the
sun, it would be the best grand prix by far."

Address :
Circuit de Spa-Francorchamps
Route du circuit 55
4970 Francorchamps
Belgium
Tel : 00 32 87 27 51 43
Fax : 00 32 87 27 55 51

ITALIAN GRAND PRIX

MONZA
SUNDAY 10TH SEPTEMBER 2000

Start : 14h00.
53 laps of 5.793 km or 307.029 km.
Attendance : 110 000 spectators on Sunday
Location: The Monza circuit is situated in the park of the same name, aproximately 15 kilometres north east of Milan and is easily accessible off the A1 and A4 motorways. There are two airports at Milan, Linate and Malpensa. You will have to curb your latin temperament to cope with the Sunday night jams trying to get onto the motorways.

Along with Silverstone, Nurburgring, Monaco and Spa, Monza is one of the last legendary circuits still in use in the F1 world championship. The banking on the oval track has now fallen into disrepair and the cracks get bigger every year as the park's plants gradually take over. They bear witness to a long gone era, remembered with affection. Monza really is one of the sacred temples of motor racing and the fervor of the tifosi when the Ferraris are on song is incredible. The end of the race features a traditional track invasion, but last year, this tradition drew sanctions. Fisichella's Benetton, abandoned at the first chicane, was left a bare skeleton as the fans took " just a little souvenir" each. Attending a grand prix here is an incredible experience, if only to feel the ties which link Ferrari and its fans. It is the magic of Monza and it is unmissable.
For years now, the first chicane has seen all sorts of dramas. Senna in 1988 and Hakkinen in 1999 both threw away certain wins there. For this year, the first corner has been modified with a first turn to the right leading to another to the left. The aim is also to stop driver cutting the first chicane and gaining precious tenths. The second chicane has been similarly modified. A great venue in a welcoming country, the Italian Grand Prix is a pleasurable experience.

MONZA AS SEEN BY JARNO TRULLI :

"Monza is fascination. The track is not really difficut. The chicanes are somewhat demanding, but it is easy to find the right pace. You can make the difference in the Lesmo corner. The car plays the key role at Monza. The fans are warm and welcoming and you feel nearer to them here than at Imola."

Address :
Autodromo Nazionale Di Monza,
Parco Monza
20052 Monza (Mi)
Italy
Tel : 00 39 039 24 821
Fax : 00 39 039 32 03 24

1999 STATISTICS

START GRID:

1st	M. Häkkinen (McLaren-Mercedes)	1'22"432
2	H.-H. Frentzen (Jordan-Mugen-Honda)	1'22"926
3	D. Coulthard (McLaren-Mercedes)	1'23"177
4	A. Zanardi (Williams-Supertec)	1'23"432
5	R. Schumacher (Williams-Supertec)	1'23"636
6	M. Salo (Ferrari)	1'23"657

etc...

RACE RESULT:

1st	H.-H. Frentzen (Jordan-Mugen-Honda) in 1h17'02"923 at 237,938 km/h	
2	R. Schumacher (Williams-Supertec)	3"272
3	M. Salo (Ferrari)	11"932
4	R. Barrichello (Stewart-Ford)	17"630
5	D. Coulthard (McLaren-Mercedes)	18"142
6	E. Irvine (Ferrari)	27"402
7	A. Zanardi (Williams-Supertec)	28"047
8	J. Villeneuve (BAR-Supertec)	41"797
9	J. Alesi (Sauber-Petronas)	42"198
10	D. Hill (Jordan-Mugen-Honda)	56"259
11	O. Panis (Prost Peugeot)	1 lap

FASTEST LAPS 1999:

Ralf Schumacher (Williams-Supertec) in 1'25"579 at 242,723 km/h.

LAP RECORD:

M. Häkkinen (McLaren-Mercedes) in 1997 in 1'24"808 at 244, 929 km/h.

RACE HISTORY

1999: H.-H. Frentzen (Jordan)
1998 : M. Schumacher (Ferrari)
1997 : D. Coulthard (McLaren)
1996 : M. Schumacher (Ferrari)
1995 : J. Herbert (Benetton)
1994 : D. Hill (Williams)
1993 : D. Hill (Williams)
1992 : A. Senna (McLaren)
1991 : N. Mansell (Williams)
1990 : A. Senna (McLaren)

Nelson Piquet won this race 4 times. (1980, 83, 86 and 87).
Juan Manuel Fangio (1953, 54 and 55), Stirling Moss (1956, 57 and 59), Ronnie Peterson (1973, 74 and 76) and Alain Prost (1981, 85 and 89) all won in Italy on three occasions.
Giuseppe Farina won the first Italian Grand Prix to count towards the world championship on 3rd September 1950 at Monza.
2000 will be the 51st Italian Grand Prix. It has always been run at the Autodromo di Monza except for 1980 when it was held at Imola.

UNITED STATES GRAND PRIX
SUNDAY 24TH SEPTEMBER 2000
INDIANAPOLIS

1999 STATISTICS

START GRID:

1st
2
3
4
5
6

RACE RESULT:

1st
2
3
4
5
6
7
8

FASTEST LAPS 1999:

RECORD DU LAPS:

RACE HISTORY

1991 : A. Senna (McLaren)
1990 : A. Senna (McLaren)
1989 : A. Prost (Ferrari)
1988 : A. Senna (McLaren)
1987 : A. Senna (Lotus)
1986 : A. Senna (Lotus)
1985 : K. Rosberg (Williams)
1984 : N. Piquet (Brabham)
1984 : K. Rosberg (Williams)
1983 : J. Watson (McLaren)
1983 : M. Alboreto (Tyrrell)
etc...

Ayrton Senna, the king of the street circuits won five USA Grands Prix (1986, 87, 89, 90 and 91).
Bruce McLaren won the first USA Grand Prix at Sebring on 12th December 1959 at the wheel of a Cooper-Climax.

In the long history of F1, there has never such a long gap between USA Grands Prix. On the other hand, in 1982, we had three grands prix, Detroit, Long Beach and Dallas all run in the same year. 2000, without counting the 500 Mile races in the Fifties, will be the 44th running of the USA Grand Prix, as detailed below.

- Sebring   Once (1959)
- Riverside   Once(1960)
- Watkins   Glen 20 times (from 1961 to 80)
- Long Beach   8 times (from 1976 to 83)
- Las Vegas   Twice (1981 and 82)
- Detroit   7 times (from 1982 to 88)
- Dallas   Once (1984)
- Phoenix   3 times (from 1989 to 91)

Start : 14h00 locale time, 21h00 in Europe.
73 laps of 4.195 km or 306.235 km.
Location: Indianapolis is the capital of the state of Indiana, situated in the American Midwest in the area of the Great Lakes. The famous oval circuit which has now been joined by a purpose built F1 track, is about ten kilometres from the town centre of Indianapolis in its western suburb. This city of 300,000 is 300 kilometres to the south east of Chicago and 400 kilometres north east of St. Louis.

The last United States Grand Prix dates back to 1991 in Phoenix in the American west. Since then, all sorts of crazy projects have been put forward for staging the next one at Dallas, San Francisco or Las Vegas. Then, thanks to the determination of the Indianapolis circuit owner Tony George and Bernie Ecclestone, an agreement was reached to build a circuit in the centre of the famous Indy oval. Now, we must wait and see if the American public has any interest in this foreign world of Formula 1. There are no local drivers or teams involved. When the 500 Miles race is on, which they rate as the most important motor race in the world, 350,000 Americans turn up to sit around the "Brickyard."
The first race was run in 1911.
From 1950 to 1961, Indianapolis counted towards the Formula 1 world championship, even though the cars and drivers were exclusively American. Although the Indycar series has now been split into two rival factions; Cart and the International Racing League, Indianapolis is as prestigious as ever. How many people will turn up for the Formula 1 USA GP?
Jacques Villeneuve, from neighbouring Canada, who won here in 1995, will no doubt be a favourite with the crowd. If you can afford it then make the journey. It is bound to be a unique experience sitting in the stands at Indy.

INDIANAPOLIS AS SEEN BY JARNO TRULLI :

"Actually, it will all depend on the track and the reaction of the crowd. The American spectators will play a key role in the success of this grand prix. I like the USA. And after all, the race is set in the home of American racing at Indianapolis. It should be quite a weekend!"

Address :
Indianapolis Motor Speedway
4790 west, 16th street.,
Indianapolis
IN46222 USA
Tél : 00 1 317 481 85 00
Fax : 00 1 317 484 64 82

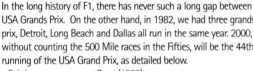

JAPANESE GRAND PRIX

SUZUKA

SUNDAY 8TH OCTOBER 2000

Start : 14 h30 local time, 07h30 in Europe.
53 laps of 5.862 km or 310.476 km.
Attendance in 1999: 146 000 spectators on Sunday.
Location: The circuit is 500 kilometres to the south west of Tokyo, 150 kilometres east of Osaka and 70 kilometres from Nagoya. With just a few exceptions, hotel rooms are tinier than the cells in a monastery. You have the option of opening your suitcase or walking to the bathroom!

It is not a good idea to plan on spending time in your room as you will develop claustrophobia. The circuit is part of Suzuka Circuitland, Honda's amusement park. It was built to entertain the families of the workers in the nearby factory. It is like finding yourself on another planet. Since the death of Ayrton Senna and Honda's withdrawal from the sport and despite the odd appearance from Japanese drivers, interest in Formula 1 is on a downward spiral. There will not be a single Japanese driver on the grid this season.

Not so long ago, ticket allocations for the grand prix were decided by lottery to see who would be allowed to buy tickets and the grand prix was a 150,000 spectator sell-out. Two thirds of those who applied had to make do with watching the event on television. The lucky winners would then sleep on the pavement outside the entrance gates to the circuit. These days, anyone can get in. Now that Honda is back with BAR and Toyota is on its way, the next few years should see a return to the old days in terms of Formula 1's popularity in Japan after a difficult few years. At last year's race a giant banner done out in the colours of the rising sun, declared "We shall dominate in the 2000 years." We shall see.

SUZUKA AS SEEN BY JARNO TRULLI :

"I do not like this circuit very much. However, I love the atmosphere. The Japanese are really keen fans. They love F1 and are like happy children at the track. Suzuka is a tough track, no doubt one of the most demanding of the year."

Address :
Suzuka Circuit G.P. Office
7992 Ino-Cho, Suzuka-Shi
Mie-Ken 51002
Japan
Tel : 00 81 593 70 11 11
Fax: 00 81 593 70 18 18

1999 STATISTICS

START GRID:

1st	M. Schumacher (Ferrari)	1'37"470
2	M. Häkkinen (McLaren-Mercedes)	1'37"820
3	D. Coulthard (McLaren-Mercedes)	1'38"239
4	H.-H. Frentzen (Jordan-Mugen-Honda)	1'38"696
5	E. Irvine (Ferrari)	1'38"975
6	O. Panis (Prost-Peugeot)	1'39"623

etc...

RACE RESULT:

1st	M. Häkkinen (McLaren-Mercedes) in 1h 31'18"785	204,086 km/h
2	M. Schumacher (Ferrari)	5"015
3	E. Irvine (Ferrari)	1'35"688
4	H.-H. Frentzen (Jordan-Mugen-Honda)	1'38"635
5	R. Schumacher (Williams-Supertec)	1'39"494
6	J. Alesi (Sauber-Petronas)	1 lap
7	J. Herbert (Stewart-Ford)	1 lap
8	R. Barrichello (Stewart-Ford)	1 lap
9	J. Villeneuve (BAR-Supertec)	1 lap
10	A. Wurz (Benetton-Playlife)	1 lap
11	P. Diniz (Sauber-Petronas)	1 lap
12	R. Zonta (BAR-Supertec)	1 lap
13	P. de la Rosa (Arrows)	2 laps
14	G. Fisichella (Benetton-Playlife)	6 laps

FASTEST LAPS 1999:

Michael Schumacher (Ferrari): 1'41"319
at 208,355 km/h.

LAP RECORD:

Heinz-Harald Frentzen (Williams-Renault) in 1997 in
1'38"942 at 213,361 km/h.

RACE HISTORY

1999 : M. Häkkinen (McLaren)
1998 : M. Häkkinen (McLaren)
1997 : M. Schumacher (Ferrari)
1996 : D. Hill (Williams)
1995 : M. Schumacher (Benetton)
1994 : D. Hill (Williams)
1993 : A. Senna (McLaren)
1992 : N. Mansell (Williams)
1991 : G. Berger (McLaren)
1990 : N. Piquet (Benetton)
etc...

M. Hakkinen (1998 and 99), M. Schumacher (1995 and 97), D. Hill (1994 and 96), A. Senna (1988 and 93) and G. Berger (1987 and 91) have all won the Japanese Grand Prix twice. Mario Andretti won the first Japanese Grand Prix at Mont Fuji driving a Lotus on 24th October 1976.

2000 will be the 16th running of the Japanese Grand Prix.
- It has been held twice at Mont-Fuji in 1976 and 77.
- since 1987, it has always been run at Suzuka.

MALAYSIAN GRAND PRIX
SUNDAY 22ND OCTOBER 2000
SEPANG

1999 STATISTICS

START GRID:

1st	M. Schumacher (Ferrari)	1'39"688
2	E. Irvine (Ferrari)	1'40"635
3	D. Coulthard (McLaren-Mercedes)	1'40"806
4	M. Häkkinen (McLaren-Mercedes)	1'40"866
5	J. Herbert (Stewart-Ford)	1'40"937
6	R. Barrichello (Stewart-Ford)	1'41"351

etc...

RACE RESULT:

1st	E. Irvine (Ferrari)	in 1 h36'38"494
		192,682 km/h.
2	M. Schumacher (Ferrari)	1"040
3	M. Häkkinen (McLaren)	9"743
4	J. Herbert (Stewart-Ford)	17"538
5	R. Barrichello (Stewart-Ford)	32"296
6	H.-H. Frentzen (Jordan-Mugen-Honda)	34"884
7	J. Alesi (Sauber-Petronas)	54"408
8	A. Wurz (Benetton-Playlife)	1'00"934
9	M. Gene (Minardi-Ford)	1 lap
10	A. Zanardi (Williams-Supertec)	1 lap
11	G. Fisichella (Benetton-Playlife)	4 laps

LAP RECORD:

M. Schumacher (Ferrari) : 1'40"267 at 198,980 km/h

Start : 15h00 local time, 09h00 in Europe.
55 laps of 5.557 km or 305.635 km.
Attendance : 75 000 spectators on Sunday.
Location: Sepang circuit is in the south of the Malaysian peninsula, 60 kilometres to the south of the capital, Kuala Lumpur and to the west of Seremban. The international airport is 5 kilometres from this ultra modern complex, linked by a special motorway.

Malaysia wants to put itself on the world map. The government thought that Formula 1 would be an excellent propaganda vector to promote this young and rich country. The oil company Petronas is proud of having opened its head office in the Twin Towers of Kuala Lumpur, the tallest buildings in Asia. It has also been a sponsor of the Sauber team since 1996.
The Sepang circuit and its organisation has made the Malaysian Grand Prix the F1 benchmark. All the other circuits in the world now appear old by comparison with this ultra-modern and futuristic facility. While it has succeeded on this front, the event now has to attract local spectators. Last year, 75% of the crowd was made up of foreigners. The ticket price is definitely the reason for the lack of Malaysians in the crowd. Last year's event was somewhat marred by the disqualification of the two Ferraris and the row that ensued. Philippe Gurdjian is the man behind the project and he is now turning his attention to Paul Ricard at the Castellet. There should soon be a Sepang-style complex in Europe if all goes to plan. A new generation of race tracks is on the way.

RACE HISTORY

1999 : E. Irvine (Ferrari)

2000, will see the second staging of the Malaysian Grand Prix.

SEPANG AS SEEN BY JARNO TRULLI :

"It is not a bad circuit. There is not enough grip though and it is not really demanding, either in terms of setting up the car or in terms of driving. I really don't like the humidity and there was no atmosphere last year."

Address :
Sepang International Circuit
Sdn.Bhnd(SIC) Wisma Bintang
Lot 13 A, Jalan 225
46100 Petaling Jaya Selangor
Darul Ehsan
Malaysia
Tel : 00 603 755 55 55
Fax : 00 603 755 73 19

STATISTICS

All statistics go up to 31st December 1999.

The ever increasing number of grands prix contested has had a slightly misleading effect on some of the statistics. The number of events today means it is easier to climb up the charts. Nevertheless, this is in no way meant to detract from the worth of the modern day drivers, who reap the benefits of Formula One's current excellent state of health.

Evolution of the attribution of points in the world championships

From 1950 to 1959 : 8 points for 1st, 6 points for 2nd, 4 points for 3rd, 3 points for 4th, 2 points for 5th and 1 point for fastest lap. In 1960, the point for fastest lap was withdrawn and a point given for 6th place.
From 1961 to 1990, the winner was given an extra point (9 points). Since 1991, the winner gets 10 points, to favour the bold and to make the maths simpler!
The idea of extending the points attribution to cover the first ten has been a subject of discussion for ages.

CONSTRUCTORS

In 1958, a Formula 1 constructors' cup was created. In 1982, it became the world championship for constructors.

1958: Vanwall	1979: Ferrari
1959: Cooper	1980: Williams
1960: Cooper	1981: Williams
1961: Ferrari	1982: Ferrari
1962: BRM	1983: Ferrari
1963: Lotus	1984: McLaren
1964: Ferrari	1985: McLaren
1965: Lotus	1986: Williams
1966: Brabham	1987: Williams
1967: Lotus	1988: McLaren
1968: Lotus	1989: McLaren
1969: Matra	1990: McLaren
1970: Lotus	1991: McLaren
1971: Tyrrell	1992: Williams
1972: Lotus	1993: Williams
1973: Lotus	1994: Williams
1974: McLaren	1995: Benetton
1974: McLaren	1996: Williams
1975: Ferrari	1997: Williams
1976: Ferrari	1998: McLaren
1977: Ferrari	1999: Ferrari
1978: Lotus	

DRIVERS - THE WORLD CHAMPIONS

1950	Guiseppe Farina	(Italy)	Alfa Romeo
1951	Juan Manuel Fangio	(Argentina)	Alfa Romeo
1952	Alberto Ascari	(Italy)	Ferrari
1953	Alberto Ascari	(Italy)	Ferrari
1954	Juan Manuel Fangio	(Argentina)	Mercedes et Maserati
1955	Juan Manuel Fangio	(Argentina)	Mercedes
1956	Juan Manuel Fangio	(Argentina)	Ferrari
1957	Juan Manuel Fangio	(Argentina)	Maserati
1958	Mike Hawthorn	(Great Britain)	Ferrari
1959	Jack Brabham	(Australia)	Cooper-Climax
1960	Jack Brabham	(Australia)	Cooper-Climax
1961	Phil Hill	(United States)	Ferrari
1962	Graham Hill	(Great Britain)	BRM
1963	Jim Clark	(Great Britain)	Lotus-Climax
1964	John Surtees	(Great Britain)	Ferrari
1965	Jim Clark	(Great Britain)	Lotus-Climax
1966	Jack Brabham	(Australia)	Brabham-Repco
1967	Dennis Hulme	(New Zealand)	Brabham-Repco
1968	Graham Hill	(Great Britain)	Lotus-Ford
1969	Jackie Stewart	(Great Britain)	Matra-Ford
1970	Jochen Rindt	(Australia)	Lotus-Ford
1971	Jackie Stewart	(Great Britain)	Tyrrell-Ford
1972	Emerson Fittipaldi	(Brazil)	Lotus-Ford
1973	Jackie Stewart	(Great Britain)	Tyrrell-Ford
1974	Emerson Fittipaldi	(Brazil)	McLaren-Ford
1975	Niki Lauda	(Austria)	Ferrari
1976	James Hunt	(Great Britain)	McLaren-Ford
1977	Niki Lauda	(Austria)	Ferrari
1978	Mario Andretti	(United States)	Lotus-Ford
1979	Jody Scheckter	(South Africa)	Ferrari
1980	Alan Jones	(Australia)	Williams-Ford
1981	Nelson Piquet	(Brazil)	Brabham-Ford
1982	Keke Rosberg	(Finland)	Williams-Ford
1983	Nelson Piquet	(Brazil)	Brabham-BMW
1984	Niki Lauda	(Austria)	McLaren-Tag-Porsche
1985	Alain Prost	(France)	McLaren-Tag-Porsche
1986	Alain Prost	(France)	McLaren-Tag-Porsche
1987	Nelson Piquet	(Brazil)	Williams-Honda
1988	Ayrton Senna	(Brazil)	McLaren-Honda
1989	Alain Prost	(France)	McLaren-Honda
1990	Ayrton Senna	(Brazil)	McLaren-Honda
1991	Ayrton Senna	(Brazil)	McLaren-Honda
1992	Nigel Mansell	(Great Britain)	Williams-Renault
1993	Alain Prost	(France)	Williams-Renault
1994	Michael Schumacher	(Germany)	Benetton-Ford
1995	Michael Schumacher	(Germany)	Benetton-Renault
1996	Damon Hill	(Great Britain)	Williams-Renault
1997	Jacques Villeneuve	(Canada)	Williams-Renault
1998	Mika Häkkinen	(Finland)	McLaren-Mercedes
1999	Mika Häkkinen	(Finland)	McLaren-Mercedes

STATISTICS

FINAL CLASSIFICATION OF THE DRIVERS' WORLD CHAMPIONSHIP 1999

	Driver	Team	Points
1er:	Mika Häkkinen	McLaren-Mercedes	76 pts
2 :	Eddie Irvine	Ferrari	74
3 :	Heinz-Harald Frentzen	Jordan-Mugen-Honda	54
4 :	David Coulthard	McLaren-Mercedes	48
5 :	Michael Schumacher	Ferrari	44
6 :	Ralf Schumacher	Williams- Supertec	35
7 :	Rubens Barrichello	Stewart-Ford	21
8 :	Johnny Herbert	Stewart-Ford	15
9 :	Giancarlo Fisichella	Benetton-Playlife	13
10:	Mika Salo	BAR-Supertec et Ferrari	10
11:	Jarno Trulli	Prost-Peugeot	7
12:	Damon Hill	Jordan-Mugen-Honda	7
13:	Alexander Wurz	Benetton-Playlife	3
14:	Pedro Diniz	Sauber-Petronas	3
15:	Olivier Panis	Prost-Peugeot	2
16:	Jean Alesi	Sauber-Petronas	2
17:	Pedro De la Rosa	Arrows	1
18:	Marc Gené	Minardi-Ford	1

FINAL CLASSIFICATION OF THE CONSTRUCTORS' WORLD CHAMPIONSHIP 1999

	Team	Points
1er:	Ferrari	128 pts
2:	McLaren-Mercedes	124 pts
3:	Jordan-Mugen-Honda	61 pts
4:	Stewart-Ford	36 pts
5:	Williams-Supertec	35 pts
6:	Benetton-Playlife	16 pts
7:	Prost-Peugeot	9 pts
8:	Sauber-Petronas	5 pts
9:	Arrows	1 pt
10:	Minardi-Ford	1 pt

NUMBER OF DRIVERS' WORLD CHAMPIONSHIP TITLES PER COUNTRY*

12 TITLES : GREAT BRITAIN : Hawthorn(1), G. Hill (2), Clark(2), Surtees (1), Stewart (3), Hunt (1), Mansell (1) et D. Hill (1)

8 TITLES : BRAZIL : E. Fittipaldi (2), Piquet (3) et Senna (3)

5 TITLES : ARGENTINA : Fangio (5)
AUSTRALIA : Brabham (3) and Jones (1)
AUSTRIA : Rindt (1) and Lauda (3)
FRANCE : Prost (4)

3 TITLES : ITALY : Farina (1) and Ascari (2)
FINLAND : Rosberg (1) and Häkkinen (2)

2 TITLES : UNITED STATES : P. Hill (1) and M. Andretti (1)
GERMANY : M. Schumacher (2)

1 TITLE : NEW ZEALAND : Hulme (1)
SOUTH AFRICA : Scheckter (1)
CANADA : J. Villeneuve (1)

*(number of titles in brackets)

NUMBER OF GRANDS PRIX CONTESTED PER DRIVER

R. Patrese	256	R. Barrichello	113	J. Clark	72	P. De la Rosa	16
G. Berger	210	D. Hulme	112	C. Pace	72	I. Ireland	50
A. De Cesaris	208	J. Scheckter	112	S. Modena	70	R. Zonta	16
N. Piquet	204	J. Surtees	111	D. Pironi	70	J. Oliver	50
A. Prost	199	E. De Angelis	108	B. Giacomelli	69	L. Badoer	50
M. Alboreto	194	P. Alliot	107	G. Villeneuve	67	etc...	
N. Mansell	187	J. Mass	105	S. Moss	66		
G. Hill	176	J. Bonnier	102	T. Fabi	64		
J. Laffite	176	B. McLaren	101	A. Suzuki	64		
N. Lauda	171	J. Stewart	99	J. Villeneuve	64	Note: current drivers in bold.	
J. Alesi	167	J. Siffert	97	J.J. Lehto	62	In the 50s and 60s, the world	
T. Boutsen	163	H.H. Frentzen	97	M. Blundell	61	championship ran to less than ten	
A. Senna	161	E. Irvine	97	G. Morbidelli	60	grands prix per season. Therefore,	
M. Brundle	158	C. Amon	96	J. Rindt	60	several famous names appear well	
J. Watson	152	P. Depailler	95	E. Comas	59	down this list.	
R. Arnoux	149	U. Katayama	95	A. Merzario	57		
D. Warwick	147	I. Capelli	94	H. Pescarolo	57		
C. Reutemann	146	J. Hunt	92	J. Verstappen	57	P. Hill	48
E. Fittipaldi	144	O. Panis	91	G. Fisichella	57	F. Cevert	47
J. Herbert	144	D. Coulthard	90	A. Caffi	56	M. Hawthorn	45
J.P. Jarier	135	J.P. Beltoise	86	P.Rodriguez	55	L. Bandini	42
E. Cheever	135	D. Gurney	86	H. Schell	55	T. Brooks	38
C. Regazzoni	132	J. Palmer	86	R. Schumacher	49	G. Farina	33
Ma. Andretti	128	M. Surer	82	R. Stommelen	54	A. Ascari	32
M. Schumacher	128	M. Trintignant	82	J. Trulli	45	P. Collins	32
M. Häkkinen	128	P. Diniz	82	P. Streiff	54	L. Villoresi	31
J. Brabham	126	S. Johansson	79	A. Zanardi	41	W. Von Trips	27
R. Peterson	123	M. Salo	78	J. Behra	52	etc...	
P.L. Martini	119	A. Nannini	77	A. Wurz	35		
J. Ickx	116	P. Ghinzani	76	R. Ginther	52		
A. Jones	116	V. Brambilla	74	T. Takagi	31		
D. Hill	115	M. Gugelmin	74	J.M. Fangio	51		
K. Rosberg	114	S. Nakajima	74	M. Gene	16		
P. Tambay	114	H.J. Stuck	74	M. Hailwood	50		

NUMBER OF POLE POSITIONS PER DRIVER

A. Senna	65	R. Patrese	8	J. Siffert	2
A. Prost	33	D. Coulthard	8	G. Villeneuve	2
J. Clark	33	J. Laffite	7	J. Watson	2
N. Mansell	32	E. Fittipaldi	6	H.H. Frentzen	2
J.M. Fangio	28	P. Hill	6	R. Barrichello	2
N. Lauda	24	J.P. Jabouille	6	L. Bandini	1
N. Piquet	24	A. Jones	6	J. Bonnier	1
M. Schumacher	23	C. Reutemann	6	T. Boutsen	1
M. Häkkinen	21	C. Amon	5	V. Brambilla	1
D. Hill	20	G. Farina	5	E. Castelloti	1
Ma. Andretti	18	C. Regazzoni	5	P. Collins	1
R. Arnoux	18	K. Rosberg	5	A. De Cesaris	1
J. Stewart	17	P. Tambay	5	P. Depailler	1
S. Moss	16	M. Hawthorn	4	G. Fisichella	1
A. Ascari	14	D. Pironi	4	B. Giacomelli	1
J. Hunt	14	E. De Angelis	3	D. Hulme	1
R. Peterson	14	T. Brooks	3	C. Pace	1
J. Brabham	13	F. Gonzalez	3	M. Parkes	1
G. Hill	13	D. Gurney	3	T. Pryce	1
J. Ickx	13	J.P. Jarier	3	P. Revson	1
J. Villeneuve	13	J. Scheckter	3	W. Von Trips	1
G. Berger	12	M. Alboreto	2		
J. Rindt	10	J. Alesi	2		
J. Surtees	8	S. Lewis-Evans	2		

NUMBER OF FASTEST LAPS PER DRIVER

A. Prost	41	D. Hulme	9
M. Schumacher	38	R. Peterson	9
N. Mansell	30	J. Villeneuve	9
J. Clark	28	J. Hunt	8
N. Lauda	25	J. Laffite	7
J.M. Fangio	23	G. Villeneuve	7
N. Piquet	23	G. Farina	6
G. Berger	21	E. Fittipaldi	6
S. Moss	20	F. Gonzalez	6
D. Hill	19	D. Gurney	6
A. Senna	19	M. Hawthorn	6
C. Regazzoni	15	P. Hill	6
J. Stewart	15	D. Pironi	6
J. Ickx	14	J. Scheckter	6
A. Jones	13	H.H. Frentzen	6
R. Patrese	12	etc...	
M. Hakkinen	12	Among current	
A. Ascari	11	drivers there is	
J. Surtees	11	also:	
D. Coulthard	11	J. Alesi	4
Ma. Andretti	10	G. Fisichella	1
J. Brabham	10	E. Irvine	1
G. Hill	10	R. Schumacher	1

NUMBER OF WINS PER DRIVER

A. Prost	51	J. Surtees	6	G. Baghetti	1
A. Senna	41	G. Villeneuve	6	L. Bandini	1
M. Schumacher	35	R. Patrese	6	J.P. Beltoise	1
N. Mansell	31	D. Coulthard	6	J. Bonnier	1
J. Stewart	27	M. Alboreto	5	V. Brambilla	1
J. Clark	25	G. Farina	5	J. Bryan	1
N. Lauda	25	C. Regazzoni	5	F. Cevert	1
J.M. Fangio	24	K. Rosberg	5	L. Fagioli	1
N. Piquet	23	J. Watson	5	P. Flaherty	1
D. Hill	22	D. Gurney	4	P. Gethin	1
S. Moss	16	B. McLaren	4	R. Ginther	1
M. Häkkinen	15	T. Boutsen	3	S. Hanks	1
J. Brabham	14	P. Hill	3	I. Ireland	1
E. Fittipaldi	14	M. Hawthorn	3	J. Mass	1
G. Hill	14	D. Pironi	3	L. Musso	1
A. Ascari	13	E. Irvine	3	A. Nannini	1
Ma. Andretti	12	H.H. Frentzen	3	G. Nilsson	1
A. Jones	12	J. Herbert	3	C. Pace	1
C. Reutemann	12	E. De Angelis	2	O. Panis	1
J. Villeneuve	11	P. Depailler	2	J. Parsons	1
J. Hunt	10	F. Gonzalez	2	J. Rathman	1
R. Peterson	10	J.P. Jabouille	2	T. Ruttman	1
J. Scheckter	10	P. Revson	2	L. Scarfiotti	1
G. Berger	10	P. Rodriguez	2	B. Sweikert	1
D. Hulme	8	J. Siffert	2	P. Taruffi	1
J. Ickx	8	P. Tambay	2	L. Wallard	1
R. Arnoux	7	M. Trintignant	2	R. Ward	1
T. Brooks	6	W. Von Trips	2		
J. Laffite	6	B. Vukovich	2		
J. Rindt	6	J. Alesi	1		

TOTAL NUMBER OF POINTS SCORED PER DRIVER

A. Wurz	1	B. McLaren	196,5
A. Prost	798,5	M. Alboreto	186,5
A. Senna	614	S. Moss	186,5
M. Schumacher	570	R. Arnoux	181
N. Piquet	485,5	J. Ickx	181
N. Mansell	482	Ma. Andretti	180
N. Lauda	420,5	J. Surtees	180
G. Berger	385	J. Villeneuve	180
J. Stewart	360	J. Hunt	179
D. Hill	360	E. Irvine	173
C. Reutemann	310	J. Watson	169
M. Häkkinen	294	H.H. Frentzen	142
G. Hill	289	etc...	
E. Fittipaldi	281	currently competing:	
R. Patrese	281	J. Herbert	98
J.M. Fangio	277,5	R. Barrichello	76
J. Clark	274	R. Schumacher	62
J. Brabham	261	G. Fisichella	49
J. Scheckter	255	A. Wurz	27
J. Alesi	236	M. Salo	25
J. Laffite	228	J. Trulli	11
D. Coulthard	221	P. Diniz	8
C. Regazzoni	212	M. Gené	1
A. Jones	206	De la Rosa	1
R. Peterson	206		

NUMBER OF LAPS COMPLTED IN THE LEAD PER DRIVER

A. Senna	2999
A. Prost	2705
N. Mansell	2099
J. Clark	2039
M. Schumacher	2012
J. Stewart	1893
N. Lauda	1620
N. Piquet	1572
D. Hill	1352
G. Hill	1073
M. Häkkinen	1024
etc...	

Among current drivers

J. Villeneuve	634
D. Coulthard	575
J. Alesi	271
E. Irvine	156
H.H. Frentzen	140
R. Barrichello	71
J. Herbert	44
J. Trulli	37
G. Fisichella	35
R. Schumacher	8
M. Salo	2

NUMBER OF KILOMETRES COMPLETED IN THE LEAD PER DRIVER

A. Senna	13613	E. Fittipaldi	2122
A. Prost	12575	J. Rindt	1905
J. Clark	10189	D. Hulme	1900
N. Mansell	9642	C. Regazzoni	1855
M. Schumacher	9193	P. Hill	1715
J. Stewart	9077	T. Brooks	1525
N. Piquet	7465	D. Gurney	1518
N. Lauda	7188	J. Laffite	1476
D. Hill	6248	J. Alesi	1297
M. Häkkinen	4903	J. Watson	1245
G. Hill	4618	D. Pironi	1238
J. Brabham	4541	J.P. Jabouille	978
Ma. Andretti	3577	P. Tambay	975
G. Berger	3456	M. Alboreto	927
C. Reutemann	3309	E. Irvine	838
R. Peterson	3304	W. Von Trips	787
J. Hunt	3229	C. Amon	784
J. Ickx	3067	H.H. Frentzen	698
J. Villeneuve	2972	etc...	
A. Jones	2877	Currently competing:	
J. Scheckter	2837	J. Herbert	226
D. Coulthard	2834	G. Fisichella	172
R. Patrese	2571	J. Trulli	160
R. Arnoux	2561	R. Barrichello	85
G. Villeneuve	2244	R. Schumacher	36
K. Rosberg	2137	M. Salo	13
J. Surtees	2131		

DRIVERS WITH THE GREATEST NUMBER OF WINS PER SEASON

–9 WINS
Nigel Mansell in 1992 (Williams-Renault)
Michael Schumacher in 1995 (Benetton-Renault)

–8 WINS
Ayrton Senna in 1988 (McLaren-Honda)
Michael Schumacher in 1994 (Benetton-Ford)
Damon Hill in 1996 (Williams-Renault)
Mika Häkkinen in 1998 (McLaren-Mercedes)

–7 WINS
Jim Clark in 1963 (Lotus-Climax)
Alain Prost in 1984 (McLaren-Porsche)
Alain Prost in 1988 (McLaren-Honda)
Ayrton Senna in 1991 (McLaren-Honda)
Alain Prost in 1993 (Williams-Renault)
Jacques Villeneuve in 1997 (Williams-Renault)

–6 WINS
Alberto Ascari in 1952 (Ferrari)
Juan Manuel Fangio in 1954 (Mercedes et Maserati)
Jim Clark in 1965 (Lotus-Climax)
Jackie Stewart in 1969 et 1971 (Matra-Ford & Tyrrell-Ford)
James Hunt in 1976 (McLaren-Ford)
Mario Andretti in 1978 (Lotus-Ford)
Nigel Mansell in 1987 (Williams-Honda)
Ayrton Senna in 1989 & 1990 (McLaren-Honda)
Michael Schumacher in 1998 (Ferrari)

–5 WINS
Alberto Ascari in 1953 (Ferrari)
Jack Brabham in 1960 (Cooper-Climax)
Jochen Rindt in 1970 (Lotus-Ford)
Emerson Fittipaldi (Lotus-Ford)
Jackie Stewart in 1973 (Tyrrell-Ford)
Niki Lauda in 1975 and 1976 (Ferrari) and 1984 (McLaren-Porsche)
Alan Jones in 1980 (Williams-Ford)
Alain Prost in 1985 et 1990 (McLaren-Porsche & McLaren-Honda)
Nigel Mansell in 1986 (Williams-Honda)
Michel Schumacher in 1997 (Ferrari)

NUMBER OF POLE POSITIONS IN ONE SEASON PER DRIVER

Nigel Mansell	14 in1992 (Williams-Renault)
Ayrton Senna	13 in 1988 (McLaren-Honda)
Ayrton Senna	13 in 1989 (McLaren-Honda)
Alain Prost	13 in 1993 (Williams-Renault)
Mika Häkkinen	11 in 1999 (McLaren-Mercedes)
Ayrton Senna	10 in 1990 (McLaren-Honda)
Jacques Villeneuve	10 in 1997 (Williams-Renault)
Ronnie Peterson	9 in 1973 (Lotus-Ford)
Niki Lauda	9 in 1974 (Ferrari)
Niki Lauda	9 in 1975 (Ferrari)
Nelson Piquet	9 in 1984 (Brabham-Ford)
Damon Hill	9 in 1996 (WilliamsRenault)
Mika Häkkinen	9 in 1998 (McLaren-Mercedes)
James Hunt	8 in 1976 (McLaren-Ford)
Mario Andretti	8 in 1978 (Lotus-Ford)
Nigel Mansell	8 in 1987 (Williams-Honda)
Ayrton Senna	8 in 1986 (Lotus-Renault)
Ayrton Senna	8 in 1991 (McLaren-Honda)
etc...	

Ayrton Senna holds the record for the greatest number of consecutive pole positions. He took control from the 1988 Spanish Grand Prix to the USA Grand Prix of 1989, totalling 8 events.

NUMBER OF WORLD CHAMPIONSHIP TITLES PER DRIVER

–5 TITLES
Juan Manuel Fangio (Argentina) 1951-1954-1955-1956-1957

–4 TITLES
Alain Prost (France) 1985-1986-1989-1993

–3 TITLES
Jack Brabham (Australia) 1959-1960-1966
Jackie Stewart (Great Britain) 1969-1971-1973
Niki Lauda (Austria) 1975-1977-1984
Nelson Piquet (Brazil) 1981-1983-1987
Ayrton Senna (Brazil) 1988-1990-1991

–2 TITLES
Alberto Ascari (Italy) 1952-1953
Graham Hill (Great Britain) 1962-1963
Jim Clark (Great Britain) 1963-1965
Emerson Fittipaldi (Brazil) 1972-1974
Michael Schumacher (Germany) 1994-1995
Mika Häkkinen (Finland) 1998-1999

–1 TITLE
Guiseppe Farina (Italy) 1950
Mike Hawthorn (Great Britain) 1958
Phil Hill (United States) 1961
John Surtees (Great Britain) 1964
Dennis Hulme (New Zealand) 1967
Jochen Rindt (Austria) 1970
Mario Andretti (United States) 1978
Jody Scheckter (South Africa) 1979
Alan Jones (Australia) 1980
Keke Rosberg (Finland) 1982
Nigel Mansell (Great Britain) 1992
Damon Hill (Great Britain) 1996
Jacques Villeneuve (Canada) 1997

NUMBER OF GRANDS PRIX CONTESTED BY EACH CONSTRUCTOR

Ferrari	619
McLaren	492
Lotus	490
Tyrrell	418
Williams	411
Brabham	399
Arrows	337
Ligier	326
Benetton	283
Minardi	237
March	230
BRM	197
Jordan	146
Osella	132
Cooper	129
Larrousse	126
Lola	125
Renault	123
Surtees	117
Sauber	113
etc...	
Prost	49
Stewart	49

NUMBER OF WINS PER CONSTRUCTOR

Ferrari	125
McLaren	123
Williams	103
Lotus	79
Brabham	35
Benetton	27
Tyrrell	23
BRM	17
Cooper	16
Renault	15
Alfa Romeo	10
Ligier	9
Maserati	9
Matra	9
Mercedes	9
Vanwall	9
Jordan	3
March	3
Wolf	3
Honda	2
Eagle	1
Hesketh	1
Penske	1
Porsche	1
Shadow	1
Stewart	1

CONSTRUCTORS HAVING SCORED THE HIGHEST NUMBER OF WINS PER SEASON

McLaren	15 in 1988
McLaren	12 in 1984
Williams	12 in 1996
Benetton	11 in 1995
McLaren	10 in 1989
Williams	10 in 1992
Williams	10 in 1993
McLaren	9 in 1998
Williams	9 in 1986
Williams	9 in 1987
etc...	

CONSTRUCTORS HAVING SCORED THE MOST POLE POSITIONS IN ONE SEASON

McLaren	15 in 1988 & 1989
Williams	15 in 1992
Williams	15 in 1993
Lotus	12 in 1978
McLaren	12 in 1990
McLaren	12 in 1998
Williams	12 in 1987, 1995 & 1996
McLaren	11 in 1999
Williams	11 in 1997
Ferrari	10 in 1974
Lotus	10 in 1973
McLaren	10 in 1991
Renault	10 in 1982
Ferrari	9 in 1975
etc...	

Williams monopolised pole position from the 1992 French Grand Prix to the 1993 Japanese race, making a total of 24 consecutive events, which is an outright record. Williams also holds another record in claiming pole in all 15 rounds of the 1993 season.

NUMBER OF FASTEST LAPS PER CONSTRUCTOR

Ferrari	139
Williams	110
McLaren	89
Lotus	71
Brabham	40
Benetton	35
Tyrrell	20
Renault	18
Maserati	15
BRM	15
Alfa Romeo	14
Cooper	13
Matra	12
Ligier	11
Mercedes	9
March	7
etc...	

NUMBER OF POLE POSITIONS PER CONSTRUCTOR

Ferrari	127
Lotus	107
Williams	107
McLaren	103
Brabham	39
Renault	31
Benetton	16
Tyrrell	14
Alfa Romeo	12
BRM	11
Cooper	11
Maserati	10
Ligier	9
Mercedes	8
Vanwall	7
March	5
Matra	4
Shadow	3
Jordan	2
Lancia	2
Stewart	1

NUMBER OF GRANDS PRIX CONTESTED PER CONSTRUCTOR

Ferrari	619
McLaren	492
Lotus	490
Tyrrell	418
Williams	411
Brabham	399
Arrows	337
Benetton	283
Minardi	237
March	230
BRM	197
Jordan	146
Osella	132
Larrousse	126
Lola	125
Renault	123
Surtees	117
Sauber	113
Alfa Romeo	112
Fittipaldi	104
Shadow	104
ATS	99
Ensign	98
Italia	92
Maserati	63
Matra	61
Zakspeed	54
Hesketh	52
Prost	49
Stewart	49
etc...	

TOTAL NUMBER OF POINTS SCORED BY EACH CONSTRUCTOR

Ferrari	2358,5
McLaren	2333,5
Williams	1999,5
Lotus	1352
Brabham	854,5
Benetton	847,5
Tyrrell	617
BRM	439
Ligier	390
Cooper	333
Renault	312
Jordan	216
March	171,5
Arrows	157
Matra	155
Sauber	84
Wolf	79
Shadow	67,5
etc...	
Stewart	47
Prost	31
Minardi	28

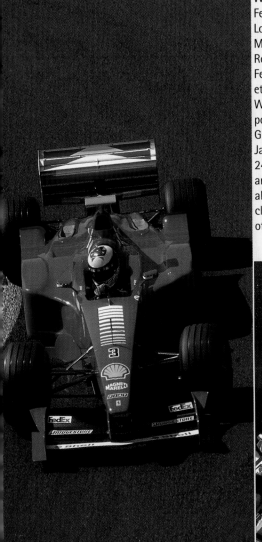

RECORD NUMBER OF POINTS SCORED BY A CONSTRUCTOR IN ONE SEASON

-McLaren	199 points in 1988	
-Williams	175 points in 1986	
-Williams	168,5 points in 1993	
-Williams	164 points in 1992	
-McLaren	156 points in 1998	
-McLaren	143,5 points in 1984	
-McLaren	141 points in 1989	
-Williams	141 points in 1986	
-Benetton	137 points in 1995	

etc...

NUMBER OF WINS BY ENGINE

Ford	174
Ferrari	125
Renault	95
Honda	72
Climax	40
Mercedes	28
Porsche	26
BRM	18

etc...

NUMBER OF WINS PER TYRE MANUFACTURER

Good Year	368
Dunlop	83
Michelin	59
Firestone	49
Pirelli	45
Bridgestone	25
Continental	10

NUMBER OF CONSTRUCTORS' WORLD CHAMPIONSHIP TITLES

-9 TITLES
Williams	1981-82-86-87-92-93-94-96-97
Ferrari	1961-64-75-76-77-79-82-83-89

-8 TITLES
McLaren	1974-84-85-88-89-90-91-98

_7 TITLES
Lotus	1963-65-68-70-72-73-78

-2 TITLES
Cooper	1959-60
Brabham	1966-67

-1 TITLE
Vanwall	1958
BRM	1962
Matra	1969
Tyrrell	1971
Benetton	1995

Note : The constructors' world championship was established in 1958.

ENGINES HAVING POWERED THE WORLD CHAMPION

-13 TITLES
Ford Cosworth1	968-69-70-71-72-73-74-76-78-80-81-82-94

-9 TITLES
Ferrari	1952-53-56-58-61-64-75-77-79

-5 TITLES
Honda	1987-88-89-90-91
Renault	1992-93-95-96-97

-4 TITLES
Climax	1959-60-63-65
Mercedes	1954-55-98-99

-3 TITLES
Tag-Porsche	1984-85-86

-2 TITLES
Alfa Romeo	1950-51
Maserati	1954-57
Repco	1966-67

-1 TITLE
BRM	1962
BMW turbo	1983

NUMBER OF POLE POSITIONS BY ENGINE

Ford	138
Renault	136
Ferrari	127
Honda	74
Climax	45
Mercedes	32
Alfa Romeo	15
BMW	15

etc...

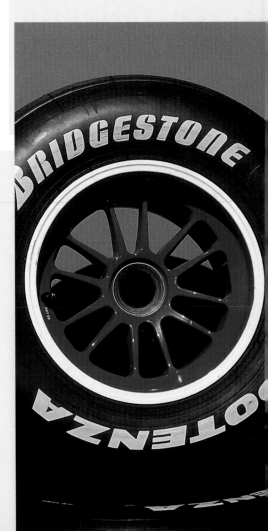

NUMBER OF GRANDS PRIX CONTESTED BY ENGINE

Ferrari	619
Ford	483
Renault	302
Alfa Romeo	212
Honda	202
BRM	197

etc...

Mugen-Honda1	30
Mercedes	119
Sauber-Petronas	49
Supertec	32

ENGINES HAVING POWERED THE CONSTRUCTORS WORLD CHAMPION

-10 TITLES
Ford	1968-69-70-71-72-73-74-78-80-81

-9 TITLES
Ferrari	1961-64-75-76-77-79-82-83-99

-6 TITLES
Honda	1986-87-88-89-90-91
Renault	1992-93-94-95-96-97

-4 TITLES
Climax	1959-60-63-65

-2 TITLES
Repco	1966-67
Tag-Porsche	1984-85

-1 TITLE
Vanwall	1958
BRM	1962
Mercedes	1998